The Job of Acting

The Job of Acting
A GUIDE TO WORKING IN THEATRE
Clive Swift

with a foreword by PAUL SCOFIELD

Harrap London

First published in Great Britain 1976
by GEORGE G. HARRAP & CO. LTD
182–184 High Holborn, London WC1 V 7AX

© *Clive Swift* 1976

ISBN 0 245 52782 6

Composed in Baskerville type
Printed in Great Britain by offset lithography by
Billing & Sons Ltd, Guildford, London and Worcester

Foreword

I like this book. I hope it will be read by actors young and old, established and student. It is always good to read of genuine experience and to have balanced attitudes demonstrated, and particularly so when they provide fresh insights into a profession so often seen through a distorting mirror. The performer's response to the judgment of critics, sometimes so unpredictably disturbing; the interesting and helpful advice to think only in the moment, when the fear of forgetting his lines is just around the corner. The part that the Arts Council, Actors' Equity and VAT play in the life of the theatre: observations which are all illuminating and positive.

There are so many lessons that can only be learned with time and experience, and often the most complete understanding must wait for that blinding flash in which we discover for ourselves, and perhaps discover something of ourselves, which does happen in the theatre. The warmth of Clive Swift's book derives not from sober advice to follow the precepts of experience, but from the clear indication of hopeful possibilities. In describing his view of our profession he speaks for himself, and because he does this with honesty he manages to speak for all of us.

Analysis of the work of actors in the literature of theatre is punctuated with the pit-falls of cliché—we are extroverts, we are vain, we are ignorant of other areas of life, we spend our off-duty hours frivolously etc., etc. All of these things are true of some of us, and none of these things is true of all of us, as with the rest of humankind. Actors are people, and 'each man in his time plays many parts', and though we have more exits and entrances than most, we do know what our roles are and when they finish, which offers us in my view a strong sense of the realities of life; and it is the absence of this sense with which we are most often charged. But when the fantasies of rehearsal and preparation are over, we are confronted with the starkest and strongest of realities, the audience. What Micheál MacLiam-móir calls the 'harsh urgency of the theatre' is with us on every working day, and if we are honest with our audiences and with ourselves, then we drop all pretences, and act. And here, if we can grasp the paradox, is a vital clue; if we act honestly, within the confines of a role, there is no room for pretence. Is this not also the experience of writers, musicians, painters, clergy, lawyers, politicians, doctors? When life in a profession is seen with open eyes we must sit up and take notice. Truth matters. Each of us carries his own theatre.

Zero Mostel said, 'The theatre is like a cathedral—at the end of it there's a cup of hot tea'. I'm sure Clive Swift could explain!

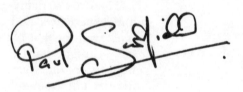

Contents

Still Running; Mental Strain; 'Camp'; Understudies; Stage Management; C.S.M's; D.S.M's; Prompting; 'Drying'; Front of House; Box-Office; House Manager; Critics; Flops

Illustrations

Introduction

Contact with Drama Students convinces me that a book trying 'to tell it as it is' is in demand. I've written this in that spirit.

My niece, Julia Swift, was a Drama student at time of writing. She greatly helped me focus on my 'audience'.

The book is for the working actor, that is to say the actor or actress (from now on they are one) who sets out to make a living by acting.

I am very grateful to Tim Wilson, Jean Bullwinkle, John Gunnell, Jennie Jenkins, Patricia Hodge, Anthony Naylor, John Bustin, Matt Mathews and Lesley Wickenden for their help. My Editor greatly encouraged a 'beginner'.

I am grateful for permission to quote from *The Professional Casting Report*, *The Oxford Companion to the Theatre* and *Understanding Poetry*. The authors and publishers of these books are in the Appendix, where other names, addresses and telephone numbers can also be found.

I would like—most humbly—to dedicate the book to the cleverness, comradeship and courage of the Acting Fraternity.

C. S.

1 To train or not to train?

**Pre-
Drama
School**

Many people think drama training is a waste of time. 'Acting is something you can either do or can't do' they say, 'how can you teach someone to do something that comes naturally or not at all?'

We are all, to some extent, performers. Performing might mean 'holding someone's attention'. We all do that from time to time. Acting resides in everyone. It's an early and instinctive means of expression. It's how we learn to live—by imitation. And yet acting is not merely imitation, many actors cannot mimic at all.

If acting were simply self-expression (nothing more), or an amusing way of keeping people's attention, there would be no need to train. (Good raconteurs don't train—though there are a great many courses advertized for 'Gaining Confidence' or 'Power Over Others!' or 'How To Make Yourself A Fascinating Human Being'. Actors must learn about that sort of thing, willy nilly.)

Perhaps *communication with an audience* cannot be taught someone who has no innate ability, and this is a large part of performing; but there are many aspects of the Theatre which an actor should be made aware of and practise before embarking on a lifetime's career. Drama School is a bridge between the worlds of the amateur and the professional.

Straight actors act within plays. They communicate with audiences through the frame of a pretend world. The Greek word for actor was υποκριτης (HEWPOKRITAYS) from which we get hypocrite.

An actor can play in any style or period of history, or the future. We can act anything that can be imagined, and not only in terms of our own 'culture' or way of life. We may be asked to play men or women, older or younger than ourselves. We may be asked to speak verse or prose, slowly or quickly, seriously or comically, standing on our head or lying on our stomach. We may be asked to sing, juggle, or execute the movements of a manual worker who has done his job for twenty-five years.

You do not always act in 'natural' rhythms. Drama is 'life with the dull bits cut out'. You may have to play in a heightened way, action speeded up like an old film (in farce for example, where worlds collide and panic is the element in which people live); or you may have to play in a mysteriously slow and atmospheric way (fear freezing the adrenalin of movement).

Is all this a 'natural' way of behaving? Can anyone do it? Look into the street. How many people walk well? How many people would you put on a stage to represent the 'norm' of human behaviour? (There's no such thing of course, but undue mannerisms or eccentricities get in the way of audiences accepting you as anyone other than yourself.)

How many people do you know who can talk clearly to a hundred others? Few. And yet actors must talk to a thousand, some deaf and blind (or seemingly so!).

Is it easy to keep your nerve in a pretend world, when the lights are too bright for your eyes and you can't see the people who've paid to watch? Can anybody do it? Is it natural to repeat a performance nightly at a precise time, day after day, twice on Saturdays? The answer to these questions is—of course not. People need to be taught a thing or two before acting for a living. Unless we can do our jobs we won't be employed; not in a society that has too many actors; not in a society as poor and as philistine as ours.

Training

Training physically tunes you. Performing is primarily a physical activity. You'll be made fit and taught how to keep that way.

Training will help you develop the actor's most important tool—the voice. A good actor has a voice of range, power and flexibility. This will not all happen at Drama School. The prime of life is a vocal prime too.

Drama students begin to think like actors. They look at the world like actors. Acting cannot be taught academically, it isn't something that can be mastered through knowledge. Degrees, honours, decorations are of no avail because every time you act you have to prove you can do it. Acting is doing. Straight acting is performing in a disciplined and rehearsed way, and being able to do so in a variety of styles.

Drama School lets you practise before loosing you upon an unsuspecting public. For that alone the schools should have more support from audiences!

Bad Teachers

If you are very unlucky you may come across (before you go to Drama School) a lady (probably) who professes to teach 'Elocution' or 'Posture' or even 'Acting'. Many of these people are a menace (I'm not speaking of qualified speech therapists). Bad teachers damn up instinct and overlay it with false manners. The law allows them to set up shop anywhere, without qualifications. They are rife in the British Isles.

Those who audition Drama School hopefuls look first for the ability to communicate emotion. If passion is displayed, or wit, or (Lord love us!) grace, there may be an imagination at work, a personality unafraid to show its inner self.

But if Mrs Pennywhistle has made her fragile talent behave like a little girl of a hundred years ago where the necessary entrées to polite society were laid down in Lady So-and-So's book of etiquette, those watching will groan and giggle and curse Mrs Pennywhistle and all her tribe. They will be annoyed that Mrs Pennywhistle has not allowed the fragile talent to express itself in its own way, to show a little of how it feels and

3

thinks about the world in which it finds itself. Bang goes a potential—Ashcroft? Ah! well, these days the fewer that get into Drama School the better.

Good Teaching

Good teachers (at the pre-Drama School stage) do very little for their pupils except open their eyes to the possibility of what the word self-expression means. They will instil self-confidence (that king-pin of the actor's life), and they will try to improve any weak physical tendency (though it's remarkable how many of our leading actors do not walk well). They will

An audition—Mrs Pennywhistle's fragile talent

4

also try to improve bad diction (though imperfect diction has been a characteristic of actors down the centuries). Perhaps acting is proving that you can walk and talk at all!

An actor should have a range of accents. If your native noise is all powerful it will limit your opportunities for wo᷉ This is not snobbery. Theatre reflects society and in socie᷉ people talk in many ways. The more people you can sound like the better. You should have a 'straight' voice (BBC Radio 4?) —unless you want to specialize in dialect(s); but it would be hard to make a case for playing Hamlet in a Durham accent. Danish would be easier!

A good teacher will enhance your love of acting, which, at an early stage, means expanding your imagination and letting the work of great writers filter through it. You will open yourself to a thousand ways of how the world appears.

Vive Le Sport

Acting is a sport. Even when you are a jaded professional it helps to look at it that way. Play, players, playing. On stage you must be ready to move like a tennis player on his toes. Your concentration must be keen, your reflexes sharp (something might go wrong). Your body and mind are in top gear, the chase is on. Acting is energy. In the theatre people pay to see energy.

You are the spokesman for your character, you put his case. Are you going to win or lose? There'll be no Drama if you look like a loser at the outset. Actors are in league, not against the audience, but with each other to fool the audience. They trick them, keep them in suspense, play with them. Sometimes they don't pretend, sometimes time stands still.

Drama Schools' Situation

1974 saw a committee formed by the Calouste Gulbenkian Foundation (an important worldwide Patron on the Arts) review Drama training in this country. Drama Schools have not had the status of 'further education' that Art Colleges and Music Academies have had. Consequently they've not benefited from public money in the same way. They have had to rely

5

upon the grants that Local Authorities have bestowed upon Drama School entrants; and they've got income from fees. The result has been that many schools have foundered. Some have found life-belts in the form of amalgamation with more secure establishments, others have found bequests and other magic means of staying alive. Without injections of cash from interested and kindly bodies some of the best schools would have collapsed.

Sixteen schools comprise the 'Conference of Drama Schools' (recognized as the best), but there are forty full-time schools advertized in the pages of *Contacts* (available from 'The Spotlight').

At last Drama training has been taken seriously.

Students leaving Drama School often face a 'realer' world than do some who leave Art School: those who emerge at the end of their Drama course usually get some kind of work in their first professional year.

In the 1960s Britain boasted perhaps the best Theatre in the world (that was the cry on critics' lips). Now we have lost some ground, and it must partly be to do with the shameful way we have ignored our Drama Schools, as though they were dubious places whose existence could not be fully justified. We have enjoyed the prestige (and the tourists' cash) British Theatre has brought, but only lately have we considered how such a harvest might be nourished. The Postscript to this book is cheering news.

Critique of the Schools

The overriding fault with the Drama Schools at the moment is that they are too removed from professional life. They are still geared to a structure that makes actors passive employees. The profession is changing fast and will change more. Our weak economy has turned much topsy-turvy. Social change changes Theatre.

Drama Schools have yet fully to realize the ways in which the actor's life and livelihood have changed over the past fifteen years. They transfuse the profession with new blood annually,

6

but this is not always the shot in the arm it should be. Schools should be ahead of the times not behind them.

Their dilemma is how best to equip their students. Should they train them for the present conglomeration that is the entertainment industry or should they make them high-priests of art? There are fundamental requirements and skills a straight actor must have; if he possesses these and sharpens them he is equipped for his trade. He must (and will) learn more, learn all the time—but the question of what sort of actor he will be, time and events usually answer.

The split that our society seems blatantly to be undergoing, that shift from ordered, structured, traditional ways, Western ways, Capitalist ways, to more Bohemian (in the gypsy sense), cheaper, more aggressive, more self-critical ones, is reflected in the plight of Theatre.

It is not easy to equip the actor to do his job at the moment. What is his job?

It is tempting (and true) to say *acting is you*. Finally it is, always it is. Perhaps schools can only instil the virtues of clear talk, physical relaxation etc. And yet Tradition (in the form of the classics?) cannot be wholly lost; though iconoclasm seems all pervading just now.

What the schools should do is to make clear to students the reality of what happens to the actor in a society as precarious-seeming as ours. I believe the actors' relation to society should form a big part of Drama training. The process of acting, of putting on Theatre etc, should be clearly shown against a real professional background—budgets and box offices; and the relevance of what's on the stage to the human life off it.

Why is there no school [so far as I'm aware] that runs a theatre—that tries at least to put students through a real situation, where tyro managers and administrators could do their best or worst, where audiences must be won, and where designers, stage-management and writers could learn their jobs in a 'real' context?

Classes (textual, movement, etc) need not, indeed should not, be dispensed with; but they might relate more precisely to what is happening on the stage.

The student-actors would live in a more real world and would respond in useful ways to it. Who knows what would emanate—what visions, to sustain the profession, would be glimpsed?

Our business is always, finally, about performing. We performers have our future very much in our own hands.

At School

Schools put actors in a humiliating position. This is partly inevitable, but some schools quite deliberately 'break down' students in their first year.* As in the Army, the new intake is shorn of much individuality, many defences. The egos are asked to serve an end which is bigger than any of them—*Theatre*.

This tussle between the ego and fulfilling a function grates. What is acting? you may ask, Am I a cog in a machine? There are times when school will seem no different from working on an assembly line at Fords. Black-tighted or masked, moving about incognito, being part of a Greek chorus or forming a triumphal arch for a wedding ceremony, you are one of a team, the focus on the whole.

Ensemble Playing

The best Theatre is produced by the best team. Michel Saint Denis (who died in 1971) said there was no virtue in ensemble playing for it's own sake, there may be twelve bad actors gathered together! The Chichester Festival Production of *Uncle Vanya* in 1963 is a memorable example of 'stars' playing ensemble (Redgrave, Olivier, Adrian, Plowright). Peter Wood's production of *The Iceman Cometh* in 1958 was another (this time without such famous names, but on a high enough level to stay indelibly in the heart). Perhaps you saw O'Neill's *A Long Day's Journey Into Night* at the National Theatre in 1972? There was a remarkable ensemble! (Olivier, Cummings, Quilley, Pickup). The best acting is the best acting (and all the craft and disci-

---

* Don't go straight from school to Drama School: taste the world first.

pline it entails). Professionally we have to be part of a team. We play our parts and we play the play. The cult of the 'personality' in the Theatre is for audiences, not for us. 'Stars' arise (people who draw attention to themselves more than others), and you may want to be one, but all you can do about it is to act as well as you know how. In the Theatre, top people come about through dedication and hard work. Plus the desire.

Attitudes to School

Don't let ambition get in the way of learning at school. There will be days when you will not feel creative. You cannot sparkle all the time, but you can use rehearsal no matter how weary you feel. You can use classes in all sorts of ways, even if you cannot concentrate 100 per cent, even if you're not outwardly contributing. Teachers may demand signs of willingness, but you are not there simply to please teacher. Learn. Absorb. Watch. Ruminate. Discover.

Nothing need be wasted upon an actor. The more life he soaks up the more he'll have to offer.

Success at Drama School doesn't mean a thing. Today's prize-winners are tomorrow's unemployed. Beware praise of any kind, although we need it like we need water. You will soon see that it is a question of the job well or ill done. You are your own best critic—only you will know (like the painter, Turner) how far off your own goal you are.

Using School

Drama Schools put you under intense pressure, inevitably you compete. You think the Principal's favour the most important thing in the world. You are torn apart wanting to do what everyone asks of you (it is our nature to please). Much activity does not mean worthwhile activity. It is better to do a few things that have been absorbed than much scantily.

You are at school to learn, to learn a way of approaching your professional work. These days an actor may be asked to act in radio or films or television or on the stage, and in any style, comical, historical, pastoral-historical-comical, as Polonius says. A tremendous amount is asked of an actor now. This is good because we have many ways by which to earn a living, but it is demanding. Think of the differences between what is required in the different media. (A performer easily becomes a jack-of-all-trades.)

You may have to be selfish at school. You must put yourself first. What do you have to offer when the moment comes, the light's in your eyes? 'A Star's afternoon belongs to the public'. That means rest. Perhaps you don't want to be a star? Still rest. We live most keenly upon the stage, that's why we're there. Life and work tug at each other, always will. Which is which? It's not always clear.

Amidst the hurly you need a 'still centre', that is what enables you to be yourself in front of a thousand people. Can you switch on and off, no matter who demands your attention?

Eat properly. Relax (sit with your feet above your heart). Cat-nap. Are you good at re-charging yourself? It's more important than a great deal else. Sir John Martin Harvey told Sir John Clements and Sir John Clements has told many people that 'Genius in the Theatre is Energy'. What feeds that energy? How can we have access to it?

'Criticism'

Actors at Drama Schools are trapped. They live with a bunch of critics! Not only staff but the other students are encouraged to criticize. Too much of it goes on. Criticism is the easiest thing in the world. The strengths of an actor must be encouraged not his weaknesses. Performance is exposure. It is our self that is being criticized.

There is useful criticism. One can learn, one can be taught; but it is unfortunate when the actor has to live in an over-critical atmosphere. Sometimes he feels he is only there to be shot down. That isn't good for anyone. The actor isn't a sitting duck for people's spleen. Professionally he needs to think very well of himself.

Leaving

Those who survive Drama School until the end are those who need to act. Schools weed out some students during courses and others give up before the end. If 50 per cent of the initial intake stay the pace it is enough: most of those might sniff work on leaving. At the moment the repertory theatres have a quota of two newcomers a year.

Do not wait until your last appearance before asking, begging (dragging?) someone to see you act. You cannot rely on your last part being right for you (though schools do what they can). The production may not be right, your performance may not be right. Whenever you are seen to advantage at school try to get someone with influence to see you. They probably won't, they'll be busy and you're not even eligible for employment: but there's all the difference in the world between people seeing you act and talking to you across an office desk.

Sometimes the question of you leaving school before the course has ended arises. Look at it this way: if someone wants to employ you, thinks you are employable, that's a plus—to your morale, to your whole outlook on the future; but finish your training. If they want you now they'll want you more later on.

Schools might do more to launch their students, their prize pupils (presumably) into the profession. Training has been but a preparation for this moment and students are too often left to their own devices as to how to get people to see their Final Shows or to whom to write (and how), or what to say to agents. This *practical* side of 'the business' is neglected by schools. The theory of everything is all very well but the practice is always different. Money should be spent on forging links with agencies or casting directors. Critics might be invited to Final Shows.

A press cutting is of inestimable value to a work-seeker.

Unless students enter the profession with a small fanfare how can they possibly draw attention to themselves? They will slip in to the water, a minnow in the Atlantic.

When you're a 'pro' you will watch others who are not trained (though fewer and fewer), and however much you scorn your school, you'll be pleased to have some technique. There is often an empty space beneath the energy and imagination of the untrained.

2 A professional start

To talk of a career pre-supposes a shape to your acting life, a beginning, a middle and an end. These days it's the beginning and the middle that worry us! How to get started? How to continue? The answers are luck and persistence, and outstanding work. But even when we live from hand to mouth, we must have a plan in mind, one that contains ambition as well as reality, desire as well as need.

Michael MacOwan (famous director and teacher) says you should have two objectives—a near one and a far one. What do I want now? What do I want in three, five years' time? Where do I want to be? What do I want to be doing?

Ideals are easy to mock, but they are necessary. Man's hopes are why he bothers to live, and you have a talent to look after. If you can, without getting over-vain, think of your talent rather than yourself (or are they the same thing?). Understand that you must try to feed it with the nourishment it deserves.

Like a centre-forward in the penalty area, hemmed in by defenders called Lack-of-job-Opportunity, Nonentity, Poverty, you must allow yourself room to exercise your creativity. That is why we play the game of acting. This book is purposely down-to-earth, but here, in talking about careers we must allow ourselves some aspiration—otherwise we aren't actors.

Try to learn the rudiments in Rep., in good Rep., and then try to taste the life of television, radio, and film. So much happens to us that we must be on our guard against being mishandled and our true abilities damaged. Pride in our potential, and self-belief are crucial to a career. We must prove that society is wrong to think so little of us. Read books which inspire. Carry on in your work the things that have been best said and thought about Theatre. Michael Redgrave's *The Actor's Ways and Means* is a short book which gives one the sense of belonging to an honourable tradition.

A Sense Of Permanence

Our two possibly permanent Companies are in crisis, one for lack of cash which threatens closure, the other for lack of cash to run its brand new home properly. The Russians have their Moscow Arts Theatre (and others) and the French have La Comédie Française which has existed since the seventeenth-century. We scoff at these 'museums' of Theatre but we should not. It is clear that to have a tradition of excellence, a standard from within the profession (and not from outside) gives our work a solid hub and a catalyst which may provoke Theatre made in protest against it, but which also inspires Theatre glad of its example. Without a tradition any trade, profession, or art, lacks an educative process, a means whereby hard-won knowledge and skills can be handed down to the next generation who will need them.*

Common Language

Reps. often keep the same actors for a season or two, perhaps longer. Working with people you know saves a lot of time, cuts out unnecessary formality and misunderstanding. Communication at work becomes clear. Everyone uses the same terms to mean the same thing, which doesn't happen throughout the 'Business'. Schools should teach a standardized professional vocabulary.

Trust developed between players leads to relaxed and exciting acting. Nowhere is this seen to better advantage than in a Company with a clear artistic policy and an aim which is shared by all. An actor who is a member of a Group doing

---

* This is why the Profession should play a direct part in training.

successful work, who is paid regularly and whose talent is fostered and challenged, has the life that all actors want. Some never experience it, and it must be painful to act for a lifetime without having glimpsed it. The free-lancer who has had the good fortune to begin acting in good circumstances has a grounding which will serve him in most jobs. He will see his work in perspective, and be able to stand on his own feet in different theatrical contexts.

Good Example

The style and tone of a Company is set at the top by the director and leading players. If as an apprentice, you sit at the feet of the best, you will study them hard, burrow into their ways and try to extract some of the magic brew. You will be influenced by them, perhaps to the point of parody. That's alright. Imitation is the sincerest form of flattery. But you will soon go your own way. You must. Frustration, boredom, bitterness set in if you are not given the chance to fulfil your own capabilities.

Permanent Companies make for supreme ensemble playing which is the best that Theatre can offer. Right and generous chemistries produce memorable performances.

The sharing, the binding, the brotherhood gives actors an ideal beyond their own demanding egos: not in a metaphysical sense but in a day-to-day practical sense, in a team sense.

Avoid Ruts

Permanency, though, also dulls the appetite for work, induces repetition of ideas and chokes invention. Acting the classics, even in repertoire, requires actors at their peak. Refreshing pauses from work are essential. Variety, the new—new people, new ways—are great spurs to further creativity. We can only give what we are, *where* we are in life. The human instrument (you) needs careful maintenance. Any actor may have good years and bad in terms of the quality of his acting.

Self-Help

Once you're out of the womb of school what can you do to help yourself? Who do you know? For the present anyone you

14

know in the business becomes a life-line. Are you the gossipy type? Do you frequent pubs? Are you a party-goer? The theatrical grapevine spreads like a forest fire! Make contact with anyone you can: estranged members of the family whom, you now discover, know someone who knows someone: people who don't know you but . . . people you half or quarter know.

Spotlight is used for casting in every medium

'The Spotlight'

Perhaps you don't secure the offices of an agent. 'The Spotlight' will give you free advice. They know a great deal, they have multitudinous contacts. 'The Spotlight' will act as an address for you and put enquirers in touch with you. They are a hub of the Industry.

They publish a Directory of Actors and Actresses in which nearly the whole of the 'legitimate' side of the business advertizes. You insert a photograph of yourself with your name, your agent, and any stunning announcement you wish to make (Hedda Gabler, Medea and Puss in Boots at Squelch-on-Sea?). The Directory is used for casting in every medium. The present subscription rates are:— £29 a year for a half page, £14.50 for a quarter page. If you can afford a half page take it: faces blur when the pages are flipped over. It also helps if somehow you can contrive to be near the beginning of the huge tome! (But not everyone can, can they?). For advertizers in the Directory there is another service: 'The Spotlight' keep a card-index record of your work. Only a personal 'ego book' can rival such a history. These progress charts (that's what they amount to) are especially useful when parts have to be re-cast or taken over at short notice; it's possible to see who has played the part, when and where.

'The Spotlight' also have a catalogue of special skills: they know which actors do bareback riding or play the clavichord, speak Rumanian etc., etc. This is invaluable for casting.

Photos

Don't spend top prices at top photographers, they are rarely worth it. Any photograph of you for publicity purposes must look alive, that's the fundamental requirement. It's a worry deciding which image of yourself to put into 'Spotlight'— it's got to last a year, perhaps several. You can't look sophisticated, beautiful, sexy, intelligent, and all the things you wish (mysterious? jovial?) all in one photo. *Don't look posed*. Current minimum rates professional photographers charge are £20 for an hour's session.

If you like any of the results get them reproduced (see

Yellow Pages). When sending particulars for jobs you must send about four different shots of yourself—especially for films. You probably won't get the pictures back.

'Contacts'

Buy a copy of *Contacts* (published by 'The Spotlight' twice a year). This contains the names and addresses of key people in Theatre, films and television. Organizations and managements are also given, and where to buy make-up or where to go for toupées etc.

Letters

You will write for work (or rather for interviews, auditions). Think what you're writing and why. Enclose photographs and basic measurements: height, weight, colour of eyes and hair. Enclose any Press cutting (you can duplicate these on a railway station machine). Don't tell unnecessary lies, it's embarrassing later. Enclose an address, and/or telephone number. Say what parts you've played at Drama School, and if you have a particular reason for writing to that person give it. You may favour joining one Company more than another.

Can you afford a stamped addressed envelope? (A definite requirement in time past).

If you write one hundred letters you may get 33⅓ replies. And one meeting.

P.C.R.

The Professional Casting Report is published weekly. It's not cheap (current rates are £6 for eight weeks, £18 for six months, £35 a year). It is a digest of information published daily in the *Daily London News*. This latter paper is delivered by hand in eight Central London areas for the price of £50 a quarter (very select!).*

P.C.R. gathers together information and rumour from all over. It has a supplement—*Who's Where*—which continually tracks down those in a position to cast, wherever they might be hiding. The mid-Atlantic tone of P.C.R. is intelligently

---

* So it says in the issue of 18th January 1975.

17

frank. In the same issue you can learn that—

> 'John Buchan's *Thirty-nine Steps* will roll in June,' 'Casting for single plays at Anglia is now via Jenia Reissar' and that 'Tennents will now produce Michael Wild's musical *Little Lord Fauntleroy*.'

You may also note that—

> 'Producer Marvin Liebman has returned home to New York, yet another departure from these cold shores,' and that 'The Fringe should take a look at the off-Broadway situation as a precedent. Five seasons ago there were 68 live theatres, today there are 12 . . . the result of new contractual cover which has quite simply killed off Broadway.'

P.C.R. is a thorough attempt to throw open the casting process, though it does pander to a hierarchy in the way it disseminates its news.

There can be little significant casting done by way of it, but it has no rival in trying to keep abreast of what's going on.

Auditions

The first rule of any audition is *get to know all you can about what is expected of you*. Unless you know the context in which you are being seen how can you imagine what is wanted?

For Reps, have half a dozen well worked pieces at the ready. Reps. often look for actors who will fit into a season. Try to find out what the plays are. You will give the director confidence if you seem well-informed.

Sometimes you will be asked to read at sight. You'll be given a few minutes to 'look through' whatever it is. Your hands will be trembling so much you won't be able to make sense of the words never mind assess the scene, character etc. This sort of thing is hell. Have the courage to say so. Ask for help. Don't bottle up your nerves (they'll get in the way of your voice production!). Theatre people know that actors cannot begin to interpret a part until they have worked at it and until it has been placed within a creative context. Be courageous. You'll be liked for it.

Go to all auditions. Force yourself, even if you don't know what you're going for. You may be cast as you walk through the door. You may be wrong for *that* part but right for something else. You never know who else will be in the place— another director? A writer?

A mental trick worth playing, one that can overcome excess nerves, is if you pretend you don't need the job, or that you've done it. Pretend anything to relax yourself! If you're *working* and you audition, you are better placed psychologically to deal with it. When auditions loom up like mountains out of a mist of. unemployment—that's when we get them out of proportion. Say to yourself a career lasts a lifetime.

·For Musicals you'll be expected to sing. They'll ask you to prepare something (nevertheless have a few songs of your own). If they give you a specific number do it as it's written. Don't re-arrange it or transpose it. Musical Directors (M.D.s) can be funny people, strict.

English Musicals are always a matter of great consternation for all concerned. Americans have much greater self-confidence in this field. They'll be polite.

Interviews

Interviews* are different from auditions. Interviews are when someone wants to see what you really look like (as opposed to those untypical photographs).

For Films

If you go for a film you will be stared at by a man on your right (profile) and a man on your left. The man you try to hold a conversation with will be centre, behind a desk, thinking he's God. Sometimes he isn't. Movie directors have many understudies (second, third, fourth assistants). Don't let on that you know he's not the real thing. He may be! Some of them now are very young and under-dressed.

If 'God' asks you silly questions ask him where the money's

---

* Actors ought to be paid expenses when attending auditions and interviews: certainly when no work results.

coming from to make his masterpiece. Film Companies are sometimes bubbles. If you went to the same address the day after you might not find it.

Foreign directors fly in to London for a few hours and are gone again that night. They've never seen or heard of you (even if they 'should' have). 'Tell me what you've done?' Francisco Goldblatt will ask.

'You mean this morning? I went shopping.' That's what Athene Seyler is reputed to have said to one of these gentlemen.

American actors are better at going through their paces in interviews than we are. They know they're expected to shoot the works. You're an actor aren't you? So, act.

Meanwhile, in the same room, an elderly rich man (the producer) is dreaming of his provided escort of the night before, and assistant number nineteen is looking at your nose through his hands held like a fish-eye lens. You can't win 'em all!

'Clips'

Sometimes you will have a session where you will be filmed (by a midget camera) reading your part. This is to show the director what you look like; or you or your agent may be asked for 'clips' of your work: TV Companies can provide these.

Humility

Auditions and interviews are part of our way of life. There may come a time when you think people should know who you are and your agent is keen that you shouldn't trot round seeing people (agents are very touchy about their artistes' *amour propre*). This is called 'being established' and a tenuous business. it can be! Our profession is world-wide. There is no earthly reason why foreign directors should know you, and in this country new generations of employer arise all the time. It is difficult for anyone to keep abreast of the whole scene. Actors will always have to swallow their pride and trot along to be seen and have a chat. If we won't do that we must take the consequences.

Auditions don't get easier, if anything they get harder. They are nerve-racking, consisting as they do of instant exposure

20

without the necessary preparation.

Interviews do get easier because one gets more philosophical as the years go by. After a certain age it is difficult not to be patronizing or even short with some interviewers who seem to lack either creative credentials or courtesy. But Show Business contains all sorts!

Yes or No

When you say yes to a job you have to commit yourself to it. You are employed because you are what you are, who you are. Bring yourself to bear on the world (perhaps a new one) in which you find yourself.

The only alternative to saying yes is to say no. We always have that power. This is a most important part of the actor's outlook upon his profession. We needn't do any job (people do not starve in Britain today). Grumbles, dissatisfactions, disillusion, contempt, moral outrage—these may be borne and work done. Free-lance actors are like mercenary soldiers, (the word 'free-lance' must derive from chivalry). We sell our skills to all comers but the choice of commitment is ours; and having said yes we have a code to honour.

The 'Fringe'

The Fringe—those forty or so permanent and 'bubble' Companies dotted around London and the provinces—have proved the central manifestation of efforts to keep Theatre alive over the last decade. Was Charles Marowitz at the 'Open Space' (Tottenham Court Road) the first? Certainly Jim Haines was there, at the Arts Laboratory in Drury Lane (having done good things at the Traverse, Edinburgh). Jim Haines, now in self-exile must be accounted the main influence upon the Fringe that grew up after him. That was in the 1960's when the 'Alternative Society' came about. Thank God it did. Many of the good things we've got are the product of it, the products of some original and honest thinking.

At present there are about a hundred and fifty 'Companies' which might be called Fringe, including permanent houses, lunchtime theatres (in pubs and whatever), Street Theatre,

Community Theatre, touring and experimental groups of many kinds. They range from Ed. Berman's 'Almost Free', through 'Belt and Braces Roadshow', John McGrath's striking '7:84 Company' (he says 7 per cent of the population holds 84 per cent of the wealth), the socially fervent 'Big Red Ladder Show' to the 'Women's Theatre Group' and Devonshire's wandering 'Orchard Company'.

It is impossible to blanket so many different qualities and tastes of Theatre under a neat phrase. They are varied in their aims. Some are theatrically experimental and some are avowedly political (class propaganda their selling point.)

Community Theatre

Community Theatre lies somewhere in between. It is a way of using Theatre that either heightens social awareness (telling pensioners what their rights are, for example) or takes plays and entertainments into areas which have not had them before (a genuine attempt to extract drama from the working-class, not a bringing of drama to the working-class for the sake of their souls); and sometimes it's a process that lets and helps communities make their own entertainment ('Common Stock' are outstanding with young people in this way).

On the other hand, the Fringe does not scorn commercial success, should it arrive. The King's Head pub in Islington has had *Mr Joyce Is Leaving Town* and *Kennedy's Children* transferred to the West End in recent years, and the world-famous *Rocky Horror Show* started in a very small way.

The Fringe is not only a real training ground for performers, but clearly the way in which meaningful Theatre has gone in our time. Experiment is in the nature of Theatre, which often shoots up from a collection of impassioned individuals at a certain time and place.

Beware though! dogma (of any kind) and propaganda can poison (theatrical art). It has always been true that the best art is about itself, in the last event. What inspires it is a different matter, what drives it might even be 'political'; but the thing made—the shape, the texture, the style, the imaginative ingredients—demands its own laws and makes its own demands (if it is to have any creative pretensions at all).

The vast Fringe is trying to organize itself. The Independent Theatre Council exists, though at the moment, in a gypsy way. Visit the different companies, see where your kinships lie.

The Association of Community Artists is the HQ of those keen to involve the public in creativity.

There is also the Association of Community Theatres.

'Children's Theatre' is what its name suggests. There are about a dozen Companies listed in *Contacts*. Brian Way sometimes has five on the road. This would seem a good way for beginners to learn the job. Are you good with children?

'The Actors' Company' is an inspiration of another kind: establishment-type actors (seasoned and talented professionals) joined a co-operative. The actors rule. They choose the plays. They employ directors, they deal with plans by committee. The Company all draw the same salary. They are equals (to themselves, if not quite to the public). They've done very well. In 1973 they broke box-office records at Wimbledon.

'The Actors' Company' is a good example of hard-working and caring players who are dedicated to Theatre and their own careers. They want good parts to play in good productions and are prepared to work ferociously hard.

Elizabethan actors were shareholders in their companies. That policy is always worth trying.

First Jobs

In your first job you can't go straight into the West End or act on a Number One Tour. You can't act in a television play, a feature film or any kind of commercial (advertizement) unless the management state that there is no Equity member who can do it. In other words if you're wanted badly enough it is possible to get you.

You can act or stage-manage in a repertory theatre (subsidized or commercial), or stage-manage on a Number One Tour (or Number Two or Three, in which you can act and/or understudy as well).

23

You can work in a Theatre-in-Education Group (T.I.E.), though preference is often given to people who have a Teaching Diploma (Teaching Diplomas can be attained at some Drama Schools or Colleges of Further Education). T.I.E. Groups are often linked to repertory theatres. There is sometimes a struggle for autonomy between the two.

—*Your aim must be to go anywhere and do anything (legal).*

Contracts

If someone gives you work, the most important part of it now is the contract. This is your entrance ticket to the noble profession. Take the contract to the Headquarters of our Trade union—Equity. If all is contractually well you will be given a *provisional* membership card of the Union. After forty weeks' work this may be exchanged for a *full* membership card.

Reading your contract

Contracts are legally binding documents stating the nature of the job you're undertaking and what you and your employer undertake to do for each other. Both parties sign them so read them first (the small print as well). You sign agreeing to honour the contract (and you may have to sign saying to whom money is to be paid, and also sign a National Insurance Declaration stating whether your employer is obliged to pay his share of your contribution for the duration of the job). You may also have to sign or initial any specially inserted clauses i.e. for you to provide your own diamond tiara or for them to provide a donkey for you to go to work on—you may be in the Sierra Nevada!

Read your contract. It's as well to know that you can object to the fifth part you play but not the first four, or that you have to ask permission before you leave the vicinity of the little market town you are going to work in. Strange things happen in contracts: don't be taken by surprise.

Keep your contract, either you or your Agent or your lawyer: without it there's little you can do should you want redress.

Don't sign anything you don't want to. Equity will advise. They will also provide legal aid should you be sued—but only if your subscription's up-to-date!

By Law verbal agreements are binding, but in practice it's much easier to enforce a written agreement (you need witnesses to things said). Be a little careful what you say in the heat of the moment. If at a party you promise to play seven leads at the Wiggleswitch Festival come high summer and plans go ahead and when the time comes you are in Afghanistan, there will be angry people about looking for you. Though, of course, a contract should have appeared at some point in the arrangement.

If a contract says *Esher* on it, it means it has Equity's approval. If in doubt ask at Harley Street.

Once upon a time a contractual issue went to the courts. A now famous film actor was sued by an important management for breach of contract. He had signed to do plays for three years but went away to play the lead in a big film (an offer he felt he couldn't refuse). The management took him to court because it didn't want its other good actors going away. The actor won his case. It was found that it would have been *prejudicial to his career* not to have broken his contract. That's a phrase worth remembering.

In order to get a *provisional* union card, Equity will demand a proper contract, one that is in accordance with the Union's latest agreement with employers. There is work done on the Fringe and in small theatres which is not recognized by the union. Jobs like these may earn your rent or perhaps just lunch: they are useful experience, they may lead to other things, and often they are rewarding in themselves, but they won't get you a card.

An Equity AGM clash between Left and Right

Equity

Equity began in 1930, and since then all improvements in actors' pay and conditions have been achieved by them.

There is a professional staff at Harley Street (Peter Plouviez is the present General Secretary), and they deal with all matters that arise in relation to the union: the ceaseless work of negotiating and re-negotiating contracts with employers in all different fields of employment, relations with the Trades Union Congress and Government, Legal Aid for members, life insurance schemes (and other forms of insurance): they give advice on taxation and Value Added Tax, and no doubt receive daily calls from members dissatisfied with their lot in some part of the British Isles. Perhaps at the moment their time is taken up with cassette or video-cassette reproduction—world rights, world royalties. The face of the entertainment business changes daily.

Council

The Council of Equity is elected annually from the whole membership. You or I could become a Councillor if we were keen to be one—we'd need a lot of votes and the capacity for hard and unpaid work. The forty Councillors are representative of the different elements in the profession: opera singers, walk-ons, ice skaters, as well as straight actors and actresses.

If you don't belong to Equity no Equity member should work with you.

'Subs.'

You pay an annual subscription. These are the current rates:

£12 (earnings up to £2 500)
£24 (£2 500—£5 000)
£36 (£5 000—£7 000)
£50 (£7 000—£10 000)
£100 (over £10 000)

Unless you have paid your subscription you are not eligible for any of the benefits and insurance schemes that Equity provides for its members; nor can you vote at the Annual General Meeting of the membership.

'Perks'

Your membership card enables you to get discount at some stores (Equity has a list of these places). It might also get you into Shows free (though this practice is at the discretion of the individual producing manager). Equity has lists of 'digs' which are reputable.

Deputies

Every Group that puts on a play (every Company) elects an Equity Deputy. It is the Deputy's job to collect subscriptions (on which he gets a small commission) and to be the go-between between management and the Trade Union. If you're interested in| power politics Equity Deputy is the first rung of the ladder.

The Equity office are very helpful about any enquiries. There is a great deal to know about one's rights at work, far more than most actors do know. Most of us are not particularly union-minded, we are pleased to work, pleased to get paid. We resist the detailed knowledge required to ensure that all are being treated as they should be, no-one exploited (even inadvertently). Perhaps we should be more militant than we are. We don't feeel necessary enough to press our claims or go on strike. Some of us feel that the nation would carry on very well without us and others think that what we do we do out of love (certainly because we enjoy it). Given the chance, show business people work hard. It might be interesting to see if the nation can carry on without us: are we vital to people's lives?

Politics

Equity might amalgamate with the strong Musicians' Union They will show us a thing or two.

Within the ranks of the union there is conflict and has been for some years past. Political extremes clash as they do in society at large.

'It is the right of every worker to work'—that's the battle-cry of the Trotskyites; but it is hard to achieve that ideal in a country where only 2 per cent of the population are regular theatre-goers. How can every actor work? By forcing people to watch them? (and yet there is only about one straight actor to 4 000 of the rest of the populace. That isn't too many. Television reaches huge audiences of course. To act in front of the same numbers in the Theatre as you would in an averagely popular TV play, you would be performing for thirty-two years.)

Even if there were more work for us (and at the moment it looks as if there's going to be less), actors can't work all the time. It isn't in the nature of creating roles to do it as though it were delivering the post. Acting is demanding: a long season in a big theatre is exhausting. In Russia they do not give their actors eight performances a week (but then the Russians have an almost holy regard for the Theatre. Actors are most respected members of the community there! It's a pity they don't act in more interesting plays.)

Equity has become more democratic through Leftist attacks on the way it works. Traditionally it is a conservative (with a small c) body and so are most of its members. There is a healthy (if rowdy) atmosphere at General Meetings, though bitter clashes between Council members waste valuable time.

It is right that the Council should be fully aware of the sorry plight of many members, it is right that Council should not work hand in glove with management, it is also right, to insist that union solidarity is the *sine qua non* for improving our lot.

But we stand on slippery ground. We mustn't kill the golden goose, which some trades have come close to doing. Employers are not automatic exploiters. We'd be in a poorer pickle without them. It is better to work for low pay than not to work at all. What do you think? Political activists (of whatever persuasion) would put politics before Theatre.* If you want to be an actor first, you must think carefully and constructively about how you can achieve that aim. Unquestionably you can, through Equity, influence the profession.

Agents

It is possible to get work without an agent (that's why they didn't appear on the first page of this book!), but it might be

---

* The present Council has been elected for its 'non-political' stance.

easier with one.

The nicest thing is to be so talented that agents compete for your favour, but that is rare. These days many are loath to add new actors to their books (Michael Billington's excellent book *The Modern Actor* has a particularly interesting chapter on agents). They do feel responsible for helping to get an actor work, and they won't want you if they don't think you will work: you provide them with a living as well as yourself.

There is no law requiring you to have an agent; some actors dispense with them when they feel safe enough to work regularly. Most of us have moments of resentment when small sums are made smaller and pickings are nicked from overtime, but it is generally the case that agents have their clients' interests at heart and are not graspers. When actors are on minimum salaries some agents forgo their percentage. It is necessary to have a good relationship with your agent otherwise life is very difficult.

Agent As Friend

For beginners, agents are guides through the dark wood of the profession. They are not simply businessmen. Good agents will try to help you shape a career (though at present that is not always possible). Agents are counsellors: they have more experience than you (don't choose a starter), and they have a wide picture of the profession. They know the market. They should know 'everybody'.

Psychologically they are a godsend. You feel that something is being done to get you work (even if it isn't). You feel that you have a real link with the business. You will soon know whether you have or not. The test is—what happens to you? Are you sent to auditions and interviews? Can you speak to your agent when you want? (or is he 'out' or 'on the other line' or 'tied up in a meeting' whenever you call?). The first year or so will prove him useful or no. Perhaps you can't wait that long? But don't expect miracles.

All an agent can do is to put work in your way—the rest is

up to you. Don't let up from seeking work yourself. You will always get most work for yourself.

Big Or Small?

There are big agencies and small ones. Some giants have branches in other countries (particularly America) and it is true to say that these are the ones that are most in touch. Some of them have writers and directors on their books, some of them fix up 'package deals' (shows or films that employ many artists from the same firm, or shows where the agency is also the management). Clearly the spin-off work in such an organization is considerable; though ,when it comes to the crunch, casting is done by creative people and not businessmen.

A drawback of big agencies is that you may be a little fish in a big pool. Where the fate of super-stars is handled who'll care about you and your rent? Sometimes agents wait until you're a big fish to sign you: then it's easier to sell you.

Small agents sometimes represent only a handful of performers and mathematics tells us that they must spend more time working on your behalf.

Don't sign a contract with any agent for a long time (most can be renewed annually). Who can tell what time will bring? Only you will know whether you're reasonably happy or not; but be careful about the grass looking greener. Employment will be a struggle, a matter of luck and sweat, whoever you're with.

It may be possible to agree with your agent that you must earn £X a year while you're with him. This used to be more common than it is now—but it's a subject worth raising.

Agents' Tasks

Agents are responsible for how much money you get for a job and also for your billing. They are responsible for giving you accurate details about where and when you must see people or do your work. Naturally, you will contact them whenever your contract has not been honoured. You employ them and you are their client. They represent the 'business' side of you. They represent your professional worth (artistic, financial).

An interested agent will see your work wherever it happens,

31

(not all of it, but he must be aware of your capabilities and your progress). He should know what he is trying to sell.

'Ten per cent'

Agents may be of great importance in a career. They can, by doing their job well, 'make' actors. If you are in the right place at the right time, if the right people see you when they should, then your talent may flourish. That is why they take 10 per cent of what you earn.

This notorious 10 per cent has stood for a long time. So far Equity has resisted agents' wishes to put it up. It would be nice if the figure was so handy for computing purposes that it never altered! But who can tell? Meanwhile certain agents do take more (they are not legally constrained). If you know of ones demanding 15 per cent tell Equity.

Reps.

Let's assume that you've got a contract, you've got a union card, you've got a job. It's in a Rep. A long way from home and friends. You're stage-managing and playing small parts.

You're new in a new place with new people. You haven't found yourself in such a situation before. Not in earnest.

It won't be easy. Simply because you've got so much to cope with.

'The Deep End'

Have you stage-managed before? Perhaps not. Have you been so ignored before? Does the director know who you are?

At school you finished rather a big fish. Now you're a tiddler.

Companies are 'democratic' these days, but in every Group there is a hierarchy (it's how animals, even human ones, work). You're at the bottom and you probably want to be at the top.

'Digs'

What are your digs like? They're very important (if you have a chance to use them). Pleasant digs, digs where you want to be, don't have to be luxurious or spotless or *haute cuisine*. A landlady you genuinely like is a life-saver; though many you will keep your distance from. You don't want precious morning sleep invaded by porridge. You don't want to be pressurized into chumminess when you don't feel like it. You want to feel at home. The theatre is where you *have* to do things, and if you're miserable there it's important that life outside compensates.

You may not have made a good friend. It's awkward not being a proper member of the Company and not being a fully fledged Stage Manager either. Hopefully you get on with your stage management boss.

You spend days flogging round town for props. You cajole traders into being patrons of the Arts in order to get your hands on a rug or a chaise longue. When you get back to the Theatre you are late for rehearsal. You chalk up a black mark with the director. Now you won't get a good part in the Pantomime!

In all probability there will be sympathetic souls around— there should be in a theatre, the home of the observant.

Morale

Don't keep everything to yourself. Take genuine troubles to your employer (that's partly why he's there). Acting's a job. Temporary secretaries flit from one job to another weekly. Don't feel you have no rights just because you're working in the Theatre.

It's important to feel as happy as possible. So many demands are made on us, we need to feel psychologically strong. Our business is performing. Energy comes from enjoyment. We fuel (or re-fuel) audiences, that's why they come. The best shows are ones that give more life to the audience. Theatre's the home of the life-force.

Life at your Rep. should get easier (more pleasant). If it doesn't, how much misery can you bear? You're there primarily for experience. You've got to eat up your forty weeks.

Your motivation will be so strong in your first job that nothing in all probability, will defeat you. First jobs may be worse than a great deal of what comes after.

But at some point in your career (early or late, some actors have them perpetually) you may face a breakdown. Courage! They're not as bad as they sound.

Breakdown

A so-called nervous breakdown is when we find ourselves in a situation (or situations) we cannot tolerate. If we do try to tolerate them we collapse—physically or mentally or both. That means that everything in us is saying stop! It is a good rule in life to do what people ask, especially when it is yourself that is asking—unless of course you really like suffering and want more of the same sort of thing. The art of living is to make life as pleasant as possible as much as possible. That may not be the point of living but it is the art. Hard work should frighten nobody but suffering is to be avoided, especially as it's unavoidable. Don't drive yourself too hard: it isn't worth it. Acting is you.

Perspective

Keep some perspective about the Theatre. It so encroaches upon the rest of our life that we must sometimes hold it at a distance. Acting's a job.

If you spend every waking hour in a theatre what will you know about the society you're supposed to reflect? Hamlet thinks that 'the purpose of playing is . . . to show . . . the very age and body of the time his own form and pressure'. There is a world outside the Theatre and unless we know about it we won't make our Theatre relevant.

Remember the world outside. It has rich miners spending their lives underground; it has schoolteachers battling daily with the foment of the young; it has suffering on every street corner. We must be careful not to shut ourselves away in a Fairyland and moan about our lot at the same time. Our job has ups and downs, good and bad, privileges and responsibilities, like others.

Directors

Professional directors will be a different kettle of fish from those you leaned heavily upon at Drama School. There is no reason why Directors should be teachers. It may come to pass that beginners will not be thrown in at the deep end. Some theatres may be designated as 'post-graduate' places where students will go to further their training in a real and functional way.

34

Directors here would still, to some extent, be teachers. But at the moment you are pitched in to work with any director you come up against.

The bulk of directors are ordinary mortals earning their living in a way that is meaningful to them.

In Rep.

Some resident directors of Reps, are overworked. Large Reps. produce nearly as much work as do the biggest national Companies. Boards of Governors do not always realize the extent of their director's work and responsibility. Sometimes it seems he is responsible for everything in the entire place, from choosing the plays and the casts, putting them in, publicizing them, and finally taking the rap for what goes on at the box-office. Generally though, the resident Artistic Director has administrative equals, and aides of all kinds (Assistant or Associate directors, designers, carpenters, stage-directors, and a full administrative and front-of-house staff). A big theatre tries to be self-supporting. Clothes are made in the Wardrobe Department, scenery built and painted in the workshops, publicity designed and executed (sometimes) in the office. Actors are another branch of the outfit. They are the men in the field. Everyone else works to put them there. What happens on the Stage is the justification for a theatre's existence.

Function

Directors have more responsibility than actors before the public is let in. They sign their name for everything that takes place on the stage. Any Group must have someone who, when necessary, has the last word—that is the director; and he usually has a more profound influence upon events.

He chooses the play and the cast and he creates a world (or suggests it at least) for the play to grow in.

In the theatre the director's job is not consistent. Sometimes he is the absolute instigator of the whole show, and sometimes he has little to do with it, just his name on the programme. Good theatre grows like a plant. It is impossible to say exactly who was responsible for which cleverness. Critics get very

confused about this overlapping and regularly lay the praise
or blame for things at the wrong door. But then, not even the
cast themselves know precisely who did what—which is as it
should be.

Relationship With Actor

The actor's and the director's work should be reciprocal.
It's nice when it's founded upon mutual respect. We need
directors because they serve as an audience and we cannot
otherwise measure our effects. We need them in different ways
from play to play: some parts are easier for us to do than others
(according to our strengths and weaknesses as an actor). A
great deal of the director's job is to make us feel good! No
outstanding performance can be given without being totally
confident about it. The actor's exposure always places him in a
position of vulnerability. Slights and hurts are felt extra-keenly.
Our answer is to huff off to the dressing-room and lock the door,
or do something more extreme like disappear for a few days.
We may be more appreciated when we come back! Seriously
though, the actor/director relationship is a delicate one. Sensitive directors won't rush in where they are not needed, but they
will when they are.

The director is the only person who sees the whole. He'll
try to shape the parts of it accordingly.

An actor acts because he takes life from his roles. When you
first have the desire to be an actor you don't think of directors,
of being directed. There is a sense in which directors interpose
themselves between you and your imagination, you and the
execution of your dreams.

The best directors for actors are those who establish a working
atmosphere in which everyone can give of their best. In a stage
production this is very important. The plant has to last as long
as possible. The soil must be good, the preparation thorough.
There is nothing worse than being unhappy about your performance in a run of a show. Everyday you face it.

Good actors need encouragement to do what their inclina-
tions tell them to. An observant director will see what an actor

wants to do but doesn't. He'll sieze upon the creative buds and make them flower. Directors who do this and who want to do this are 'actors directors' and are the best in the world!

The word 'Director' (they used to be called 'Producers' in Britain) came from America, from films, about seventeen years ago. It has had an adverse effect upon the psychology of those who assume the title. Too many are too bossy.

Every director should have performed at some time. The best leaders are those who understand (truly) the nature of the work. The public-school tradition of being leader because you

A Director

have *never* encountered the task in hand and find it therefore easier to give orders (ignorance is bliss) will not do. Too often productions are made to work by the actors who will look very foolish if they don't. The exercise of power is no justification for being in an important creative position.

An actor must assess his director's worth as he will yours. You will learn, in time, what to 'take' from a director (what can be helpful) and what to resist. Yours is the performance. He may leave the country after the opening night. You can't always do things because you're told to. We make the 'truth', we spin it like a web, from moment to moment.

Directors' Training

Most directors in the Theatre (where a good many of any kind start) do not train. This is preposterous. If actors can be trained so can directors. There are fewer arguments for directors to start professional work untrained than there are for performers. Directors have much more that is 'objective' about their work. They also have 'man-management' to contend with (a way of approaching people that is thought most important in other trades). Directors are responsible to all those they work with, and viable ventures should not crash for lack of an experienced director. Audiences are greatly influenced by the work of the director—they want their money's worth; they don't want to be practised on. Professional actors could be semi-employed for training productions for directors (at schools).

Self-confidence and articulacy are not enough credentials to parade as a 'director'. Stanislavsky kept his actors waiting years before they could play a part. It would be sensible to do the same with some directors.

The all-pervading influence of the director came late to our trade. William Schwenck Gilbert growled through his moustache at players who imagined they knew his lines in the 1890's, but before Stanislavsky we don't hear much of the breed.

Stanislavsky

Stanislavsky was an actor (and a director): acting was operatic when he began to stage the plays of Chekhov. He analysed what actors should do on a stage. He also analysed the actor's imaginative and physical attributes, seeing what was needed and in what degree for each role. The actor's work on his part and his work on himself—he divided our job into those two broad parts. Read *An Actor Prepares, Building a Character* and *Stanislavsky Rehearses Othello* or you won't get a fair assessment of his ideas. He has been misinterpreted by succeeding generations (as is the inevitable lot of us who deal in moments). Stanislavsky says: 'love the part in yourself and not yourself in the part', and: 'find the part in yourself'. That is to say a great deal about our job and our acting lives.

Brecht

Brecht (Berthold, wiry, intellectual, German) is probably the second most influential man of the theatre of the twentieth-century. He inherited an over-romantic Theatre. He wanted to wake people up and make them Marxists. He wrote some great plays.

What Brecht distrusted was 'that willing suspension of disbelief for the moment, which constitutes poetic faith' (Samuel Taylor Coleridge). [So does Michael Billington on page 190 of *The Modern Actor*]. As if you can control the minds of a thousand spectators! allowing no personal vagaries, no aberrations from the path of fixed common sense!

Shakespeare's theatre was innately Brechtian. It was open to the sky, unmoodily lit. The players trebled and quadrupled wearing different hats. People answered back, promenaders dropped of the plague. He had to exhort them to 'Suppose within the girdle of these walls . . .' or 'Think when we talk of horses that you see them'. 'Now entertain conjecture of a time . . .' he would say, or 'Thus with imagined wing our swift scene flies in motion of no less celerity than that of thought'. The minds of men! How can you prevent the use of their imaginations?

Brecht's imagination made his characters more fully human

than he might have wished. They move us. Theatre can't do that unless there is belief, at some point during the evening, on both sides of the curtain. 'The *willing* suspension of *disbelief*'. Coleridge is no fool. We can sit in a theatre and travel anywhere. There are not pragmatic solutions to all human problems.

For the actor there is a problem in trying to be a good Brechtian. You split yourself in two, demonstrating the character and what he did (for it must all take place in reported speech, the actor act in the past) through yourself. There tends to be a split personality in all acting, but Brecht would have the *actor* and the *character* remain distinct. They don't. The mask sticks to the face. All plays happen in the present, the play-event happens now. Brecht wanted to constantly remind people that they were not watching real things. Look at anything long enough and it becomes real! What we dwell upon long we accept (unless it has no credulity at all). The spectator is always a potential protagonist. He sits silent (in England they're so well behaved!); but if interested, if involved, remarks throng his brain.

Originators

Some directors create Theatre (even before the writer). Barrault, Brook. When you work with them you offer yourself, an Isaac to an Abraham. You are used, and there may be salvation in that. The results of startling Theatre are the wonders of life itself. Man in Nature. Natural man, presented with the greatest (tho' often simplest) artifice.

Other directors (Hall, Anderson) are inspired by the Word. The actor serves a Text. True articulacy is a great human gift. But is it the greatest?

For many actors the director is the boss, the know-all, the inspirer, the brain-box, the visionary, the dictator. There are giant directors (a few), and it is true that very often the actor's function is to embody the concepts which the director reveals through or imposes upon the piece. But English Theatre has lived primarily through giant actors. Our class divisions retained a feudal pattern: kings and heroes in life reflected 'great' men on the stage. Now it isn't so. We are all heroes or slaves. Willy Loman* (little man trying to be big) is the supreme example of a tragedy life inflicts on so many of us. Actors are level and directors are needed to arrange them into shapes.

The twentieth century's concern for detail (and the extent of contemporary knowledge) stretch the actor's traditional requirements. Acting isn't in itself an intellectual process.

Directors who might be professors or politicians or brain surgeons work in the Theatre. Why not? They try to do meaningful work through the medium of the show. Sometimes they bring wonderful dimensions and textures to pieces, sometimes they over-elaborate, over-complicate, make rational what is not necessarily so, and make literary or pretentious an art form that is at root popular.

Without actors all directors would be out of a job. Without good acting no Theatre (however brilliantly written or conceived) can have an impact. The open-minded, wanting-to-please, wanting-to-be-praised, wanting-to-suffer actor is the heart of the enterprise. He should be handled with care.

---

* Arthur Miller's 'hero' in *Death of a Salesman*.

3 The theatre

The Chancellor of the Exchequer has so far been unable to
lift Value Added Tax from actors' lives. Perhaps one day he'll
do it. There have been many and heartfelt outcries against
this penalty, one which affects both production and our personal time and outlook. We are all governmental tax-collectors
and for the actor it is a role quite outside his range.

The Government argue that commercial and 'sexploitive'
Theatre should not be allowed to profit (which it would even
more if VAT were lifted); thus subsidized Theatre is punished
and dwindling. Theatres are going dark all over our islands.
It is a depressing time, and difficult to write brave things about
acting or encouraging things about 'earning a living'. We have
never had it so bad (not in my experience). The nation cannot
afford us. Attendances in cinemas go up (as they always do in
time of economic depression apparently), but theatres are
ostracized. Only the truly excellent survive.

News bulletins tell of workers demanding higher wages.
No-one works harder than actors when they're given the chance.
How necessary are we? Not at all? The sheep and the goat
actors are being sorted out. The underlying motives for being
an actor are revealed. We must find audiences. Always we
must tell them about how our society's changing. It is clear that
the making of money is an appalling reason for acting. The
actor is an idealist if ever there was one.

There are still some theatres, where business goes on nearly
as usual, where names twinkle, where tickets are bought no

matter the price, and where taxicabs block the night streets. Let's go in to cheer ourselves up. Not in the front door of course, not down the plush carpet reserved for patrons, but behind, through the stage-door, where it matters.

Backstage

Actors have to be in their theatre thirty-five minutes before the curtain rises. This rule is sacred because the panic that ensues from late arrival throws many people into confusion. Understudies begin 'taking over'—do you want that? How will you explain your lateness away if you are met by a furious stage-manager and an understudy struggling into your costume? You don't want a reputation for unreliability among employers or anybody connected with the business. Trust, trust. The simple necessity upon which we interdepend.

A Stage-Door Keeper sits inside. A porter alright, perhaps a Macbethian one with a bottle and a naughty mind, but probably not; more likely he's a decent fellow, happy to be in his small corner, still in theatreland where he's been for perhaps fifty years. These days there are lady stage-door keepers too. The stage-door keeper and the fireman alternate keeping guard, being on call, linking with the outside world. Messages from agents, friends, the Press, the wife, the calling of cars, the giving and receiving of billets-doux, late and recent instructions from directors or management, all these are the stage-door keeper's business—for the entire Company. It is traditional to tip him at the week's end. Has he done anything for you particularly, personally? He can be useful. He can keep people away (he will of course never let anyone into you during the half hour before the performance). He can tell you of visitors, smile at your friends, banish your enemies. He is the bastion between the world and work. In an efficient organization you may have to sign his 'clocking-in' book.

Company Notice Board

Does the Company notice-board have anything new on it? Look at it daily. It concerns your fate. Not only rehearsal calls and Equity instructions are posted there, but travel arrangements and dreaded closing notices. It is amazing at how short notice you can cease to work. You have to be paid according to your contract, your money doesn't stop instantly, but work does. Of course you will be aware to some extent of how business is doing. The difference between full and empty houses is clear to any performer. No doubt you will have harried your agent for the past two weeks—or are you in a success? Let's assume you are.

A 'Run'

Commit yourself to the run, you're fortunate to come by it. Your work might only last about thirty hours a week. Many other people work more than that (but regularly of course and probably for more money).

Runs take over your life. Gradually you will fashion a rhythm of living which is geared around the evening performance. You will take long to unwind at night, probably go to bed late. When you wake up be active: take some strenuous exercise every day: make yourself take an interest in things and people that are nothing to do with the show (or Theatre perhaps). Rest at some point before the performance: you have to be at your most energetic at curtain rise.

Six months is a run and so is six years. Current attitudes towards being in a run differ from past ones. Many actors now want to be in a run as short a time as possible. Runs are a form of imprisonment; but then what do we want? A role or no? A job or not? Television has made work seem more various, more possible, faster. Imagine if there were no telly! We'd be clawing each other to get into a run.

Managements want you for as long as possible. The public likes to see the original product, and take-overs take extra rehearsal, extra costs: they also jostle the jelly (if I may so term the show) which may not be a bad thing from time to time.

Repetition brings its own hazards, through the nightly discipline and feeling of deadness it can bring. Actors vary in their approach to repetition. Some are keen to repeat precisely what has been 'set'. Their aim is to keep the show always as it was on

44

the first night. They cross off their laughs on a list by their mirror. They puzzle about the ones that weren't there. Why? Who moved? They post friends in front to see how and if things change. They have in their heads the form of the show as it should be, as it was. They must play it correctly, all the notes right.

Some personalities rebel a little at this straitjacket. Repetition can bring boredom which can only be appeased by novelty (in fact every performance is unique). Repetition also brings lack of concentration. A good deal of the actor's thought is upon not letting the mind play unwanted tricks, not anticipating moments that the whole being knows are coming, not acting from a blue-print that was sketched moons ago. It's a problem, sometimes a frightening one. The mind invents terrors to keep itself alert (fear of 'drying', faintness, stage fright —real and unreal things).

We grow, change, (get older!). How can a performance stay the same? Isn't it a physiological impossibility? Isn't it this feeling of remote control that gives 'West End acting' such a bad name? Or is this professionalism, the acme of our art? If you watch on a good night magic is made, but if you spectate on a bad night you will not be involved.

'Green' Room

Your theatre probably won't have a 'green' room, a common rest room (however small) for the whole Company. Centuries ago these places (they were painted green), were where actors and actresses paraded before and after the show and met their public. It was too much for Dr Johnson. He was disturbed at having his 'amorous propensities' aroused. These days few Companies or theatres run to a green room. In some though, you can get a coffee, a snack.

The actor's real sanctuary is his dressing-room. Hermione Gingold says she always paints hers on instalment. You can't have a clearer territorial signal than that!

Dressing Rooms

No matter who they are, owner, management, best friend, director, no-one should treat your dressing-room as public— no matter who *you* are. The actor's in the theatre to be a public person, to give out, to do battle. The dressing-room is where he can take refuge before and after the action. It might be your chapel, your bedroom, your gymnasium (though you'll probably be sharing it with other people).

Dressing-rooms vary enormously in size, comfort and atmosphere. Some are cells, institutionally decorated (or undecorated); some are new, functional, unrelaxing; some are cosy and tatty; some are grand. What's the size of the Company? What's the extent of the accommodation? How many actors must have singles?

In a theatre in Germany (where there are such well-heeled and plentiful theatres), the dressing-rooms are fifteen minutes away from the stage which you reach by means of a lift and a guide. At the Arts, Cambridge, or at the Aldwych, or the Garrick you can dress within five seconds of the stage. Where will you be? Strong legs are a prerequisite of the trade!

Wherever you are, depending on how long you are there, and especially if you're touring (for often when you're touring your dressing-room becomes a living-room), you will want to feel comfortable. All who share should combine to make it liveable-in (and they must combine too, not to be selfish in their little ways, too devoted to transistor radios for example).

Living with people while performing is an interesting phenomenon. Some like constant chat, constant activity, others like contemplation and silence. Some could not concentrate on cards for the world, others play chess, write letters and become world Scrabble champions within a month. What is the rhythm of the show for you? What are the demands made on you on the stage?

Dressers

Dressers go with dressing-rooms: not always of course, they're not always necessary. If you earn a good wage you have to pay for your own dresser (do you really need one?) If you are a middle-order performer or you're the lead (in the West End or a Number One Tour) you can have a man (or a lady) all to yourself. There are many willing dressers, they don't cost the earth. It's a useful and sociable way of picking up a few quid of an evening: students are glad to do it.

It's healthy not to feel totally isolated in a dressing-room. A good dresser (one who does not interpose his own ego between you and your performance) is a great bonus. He can be relaxing company, solve all minor clothes problems (a missing stud? Split tights?) and make the process of doing the show much smoother than it might be. After a while he knows the show as well as you do, knows when you want a sip of something in the wings, handles that very quick change with seconds to spare and guides you like a blind man to where you make your entrance (should you need such mollycoddling). If you serve drinks on a crowded first-night your dresser might like to help you host. The real function of dressers is not to be personal valets, but to look after the clothes, costumes, keep them clean and in good repair, to be a link with the Wardrobe Department, its representative where the action is. Dressers are a luxury item. These days actors must help one another get in and out of cumbersome or elaborate clothes.

Make-Up

The idea of having brightly lit dressing-room mirrors (you'll be lucky!) is to simulate the lighting on the stage. Of course this is impossible since stage lighting is an amalgam of different colours at different strengths. Make-up has to be adapted according to the nature of the show's lighting. You have to have someone out front (the director probably) to tell you if your make-up makes sense or not. The chief aim is not to make it obvious. An audience should be unaware of the lengths you've gone to make skinny-you look fat or juvenile-you look ancient. It's a painstaking business. Some actors are naturally bad at it and need help from more inventive, more artistic ones. Some are astonishingly good and will go to enormous lengths to make make-up work for them. Used well it can enhance a career, make many things possible that would seem not to be.

Modern stage lighting makes much plastering of paint on un-lined brows a waste of time. Lines do not show up from the front. What tells is the relief (in the geographical sense) of your face-jutting brows, bulbous cheeks, wigs, false noses. Make-up is so expensive that it is advisable to learn to make do with as little as possible. It depends on the part of course (all white actors need a certain amount for Othello and all black actors, presumably some for Iago). The character's complexion must be right (is he healthy or unhealthy? from Spain, Iceland or simply Scotland?); but ageing is best done by contours.

The older you get the less make-up you use because you begin to understand that audiences come to see you, the person, the personality. We can hide or try to hide as much as we like. Laurence Olivier, Alec Guinness and Michael Redgrave have, in our time, been in a class of their own as make-up artists. Guinness's screen range and a performance like Olivier's Shylock (1973–4) make astonishing use of make-up. It can work its own sort of magic, but the actor has to enliven the image.

Be careful not to wear so much beard or so many false teeth that you hide your face or lock your jaw! Hats (of which designers are so fond) are terrible maskers of faces. The eyes and teeth should usually be seen, otherwise audiences feel they don't reach you (nor you them).

The Fray

Has the 'five' gone in your dressing-room? The penultimate call over the tannoy, coming from the Stage Management in the prompt corner, before 'beginners please'? Are you a beginner? You are. Check the details of your clothes. Don't rush. Calmness is all. Acting is control, as much control over yourself, your fellows and the audience as you can muster.

'Stopping people coughing' Sir Ralph has said.

'The stage is a battlefield' Sir John has said.

Over the loudspeaker you can hear the audience assembling. Are they like the sea? Are they giggly (is it a school's matinée? Pity the young lovers!) At Chichester the holiday atmosphere comes across and on First Nights in London the feeling that the vultures are waiting seeps in. Courage! 'Act One Beginners please'.

Discipline

We first go on a stage because we want to communicate with people.

When you're a professional actor you must use all your concentration to remain within the fabrication of the play, not primarily court the audience. You must respond to your fellow actors and do what has been plotted by writer, by director and yourself. You bring set speeches and set actions alive. You make the audience follow them, make them stay with the shape of things so that what they need to know they know, and so that the slopes and peaks of the play are revealed. The cast has built something: show that to the audience.

Audiences

There are as many reasons why people come to a theatre as people who come (which isn't enough). Any audience is a collection of random individuals. It is our delight and our triumph to turn them into an homogeneous whole. It isn't easy! To begin with most of them haven't got rid of the world outside when the curtain goes up. Their heads are full of casseroles in ovens and bank balances, dental appointments on the morrow and what to get Mother for her birthday. It is nice when they're eager, excited, receptive. A certain percentage will be.

The first quarter or half-hour of a play is when the audience tunes in to the world of it. If the language of the play is archaic (out-of-date) they have that problem too; but always they have information to absorb about the characters and their lives, about the plot, about the sort of people they are to share the evening with. Never worry if, when you are playing comedy, you don't get early laughs. Laughter comes from relaxation on the audience's part, familiarity with the characters and their world. You can't laugh at jokes unless you understand the references.

'Playing to the gallery' is an old theatrical expression. It means putting the audience first in a way that diminishes the stage fiction. We do plays for audiences, let's be clear about that. Actors' studios and Group improvization and 'truth', honest subjective 'truth' is all very well, but productions must be conceived in terms of making things plain to an audience; and so must performances. There is a delicate balance between playing for the greatest 'truth' and making sure that the audience isn't coughing or that if they are your lines are heard. When an actor picks his way through coughs, when he (subli-

Audiences can be a nightmare

minally) uses the silence or the laughter of an audience and turns it into waves of thralldom or rising cries of gaiety, then you have a performer at work, someone with the right to be called a performer. The actor *is* a *performer*.

Disturbance

Audiences rustle, audiences talk; they cough, they turn programmes, they fan themselves with programmes during heat waves. They eat sweets, crinkle papers; interpret the play to one another, faint, go to the loo. They arrive late, they follow what you're saying from a textbook (and are perplexed when cuts happen). They stand at the back and at the sides, they shift in their seats, they go to sleep. They snore in the front row.

At Stratford-upon-Avon, the Royal Shakespeare Theatre's apron stage had seats at touching distance. There were exits downward by the front row. The late Patrick Wymark (prime Shakespearian), was making his exit at the interval of *Twelfth Night* (after the great and touching drinking scene). A hand was put on his shoulder. 'Thank you' said the owner of the hand. Pat said he didn't know if he was being congratulated for the scene or for leaving the stage.

Ill-mannered, noisy audiences make us aggressive. What else can we do? We feel we are wasting our time acting, the audience is so uninterested. Some actors have been known to speak to audiences (out of character) and tell them what they think of them. It is peculiarly painful when attention isn't paid to us, our *raison d'être* is removed. On the other hand we are doing a job, giving a service. We get on with it in adverse conditions. Schools' matinées can find so much of a tragedy hilarious that you may as well save your voice for the evening performance. Another worrying aspect of performing is when the audience don't think you're as funny as you think they should.

Laughter

Laughter is our most rewarding response. It means instantaneous approval. It is proof of effect. It is justification for the proceedings taking place (the actors acting, the audience paying their money). Laughter can be unexpected or absent—both 'throw' an actor, yet they're bound to happen. So much combines to make laughter take place. The size and mood of the audience (are they yet one whole?) the way you are acting, the way all on stage are acting. Was the 'feed' line audible? Did someone move? Has the evening paper come out with a headline that makes the joke sour?

Don't play for laughs but get them! A leading actress told me, 'We are not in the theatre for laughs!' We are. As much as anything. As much as tears. All good actors have a comic sense. Acting, role-playing, is to some extent a critique of human behaviour. If we do not find or cannot make some of that funny we are in a sorry state.

The stand-up comic, the entertainer, the man who tells jokes by himself, no-one else to help or mar his work—he represents the performer's lot *in extremis*. Sometimes people laugh at him (well, he does look funny, perhaps pulls funny faces, perhaps has a funny face—why, after all, is he spending his life clowning?) Hopefully they laugh with him, at themselves, at life, because sometimes that's the best thing to do. But when they don't laugh it is painful. They don't have to, they're not paid to (like an opera '*claque*'). The man is up there to create laughter, if he doesn't he can either brave it out, harden himself, get aggressive, or go away, tail between his legs (think of some better, wiser, or more obvious jokes and make a come-back). Straight actors are less exposed than this. They draw a veil (in the shape of a 'character' with his words and relationships) between the onlookers and themselves. But it's still you and me up there (no-one else). And them out there laughing or silent.

Performance Level

If we can keep them interested, keep them listening we are doing our job well. 'Acting is stopping people coughing.'

A competent professional actor builds a stage performance to a level below which it never sinks. It may rise above it,

52

depending on his mood, but it should never worsen. That's called giving people their money's worth.

On the stage, you go 'over the top' (to use a war image). Shell shock sometimes results. But plays are vehicles, they take us with them. Musicals whisk us along. Theatre is a doctor, good therapy as often as not. It gives us a jolt, forces us to come alive and to expend energy sometimes when we feel we can't. (It's foolish to try to make words describe acting. Denis Diderot—man of letters, French, eighteenth-century—said actors were the most ambitious poets because words were not enough for their aspirations, they had to make their images concrete, to become 'the thing itself'.) A thrilling stage performance is worth it's weight in gold. We make ourselves vulnerable. The best performers—Joan Sutherland, John Gielgud, Ken Dodd—make themselves wholly known.

Still Running

In your run (is it off yet?), how are you doing? You will go through phrases; through days of dullness and routine, and periods when you will re-discover springs in the part. Every performance is a unique happening (for the audience too). Actions we practise we become good at. Practice makes perfect. It's true of acting. Things you couldn't do two months ago you can now. Nuances, delicacies creep in. The performance improves. Difficult 'technical' problems become smooth; you've solved them. The danger now might be that the performance will become too smooth, mannered even. You proudly present it to the audience, all problems solved, only the finished clean-cut product, held up like a gift, something torn away from the world of the play (the context of the other actors, what they are giving you and what you should be giving back). It is good for us all to have refresher courses from time to time. Go back to basics. Cut the flummery. In a naturalistic piece (a slice of life) realness is the main thing. To continue to be a real person quarrelling with a lover, looking after Mum, giving and taking as in life, openness is all; remaining open to the moment and what the other actors are doing to you. Acting is re-acting.

You shouldn't know what you're going to say next, and then the words, the writer's words, come when you need them.

Actors working represent the individual who is forced to respond to the world. (Like Stanley in Pinter's *The Birthday Party*). We can't stay silent, walk away, there'd be no play. Sometimes we must dredge up from the depths of ourselves words we don't want to say, tears we don't want to cry. Daily at seven-thirty. The actor is a sufferer alright. The things he does for a living!

Mental Strain

We're in an extraordinary trade. Think of an aunt, think of a friend—do they act? Would they dream of being actors? Why not? There are a thousand ways in which to live life, in which to do the things you want, to fulfil yourself. Why do we put ourselves under such pressure? Why do we demand so much of ourselves?

Keep it in perspective. Place yourself in society. Unless you keep measuring yourself against life and the world you will be a prey to odd states of mind.

Acting interferes with the mind: schizophrenia, paranoia and megalomania (to name but a few psychoanalytical terms for what goes on in the chemistry of the brain) happen to us *and to people who are not actors*. We are not peculiarly special. We are as other men are (to echo Bottom the Weaver). We do a different job. It has its hazards.

It would be interesting to compare these 'hazards' with other trades. Everyone uses themselves in their work. No matter what job you do—concert pianist, surgeon, lorry driver. It's as well to keep fit, to be at your best (life's better that way, more enjoyable—it's not only a question of efficiency); but perhaps no other job demands quite the personal discipline of performing. You say to people 'Look at me, watch me, aren't I wonderful? I can do—anything!' We don't just boast (because good actors deliver the goods, great ones have *achieved* greatness). Self-mastery. Nothing more nor less. Ambitious actors fly in the face of the sun, like Daedalus.

They are trying to say—'I am master of myself'. And yet they are human (only too human).

Yoga, Zen Buddhism, the 'Alexander' technique, Meditation, actors are into all these, and justifiably. (Religion even! Actors have been known to take to such things!) We are instruments and we are human. Western Theatre has the face of the human individual. Other traditions are more abstract. Gordon Craig favoured masks (Greek actors wore them).

Are we a person, you, me, with wives, children, addresses, who shop at Sainsbury's—or what are we? You may be pre-

Your dresser at a TV Centre

tending to be someone called Atahualpa in *The Royal Hunt of the Sun*. Or a seventeenth-century bard who speaks prose so salacious and stylish that in Marks and Spencer of a morning she's quite lost for words to communicate with the assistants.

'Camp'

'Campness' is a way of looking at and dealing with our lives that manages to embrace such collisions—the collisions of existence that we continually encounter as actors. Being camp is a safety device, perhaps a philosophy. It may stop us from going mad. We take lightly what others take gravely. Camp is an attitude towards the world (it can exist on the highest intellectual plane) which reflects the briefness of things. In actors it reflects their sense of impermanence. It is difficult to take the material world seriously and more difficult to take serious people seriously. The roof may fall in, the heart stop beating. Live. Express. Excite. Be excited. Give. Be jolly. Be daring.

It is said that long-range thinking is a sign of man's highest intellectual potential: foresight, planning, the ability to wait for reward. Acting induces the opposite: living for the moment.

Understudies

Understudies are required for plays that run. In Rep. there is not time (nor hopefully the need) to 'cover' parts. If someone is ill they play: if they can't possibly, some emergency measure has to be taken—an A.S.M. goes on reading from the prompt copy which will show exactly what to do.

In a run or in 'repertoire' (when more than one play is being given) all parts are usually covered. Officially understudies must be prepared to go on opening night: unofficially they'll be in a dreadful state if they do! (and so will the world). Productions are not complete until the first night (not even then sometimes). Leading players will play the opening night, even if they're never seen again in the role. Cancellation of the opening night causes such a pother, such disruption in Press and Publicity (in relations' time-tables and critics' good-will) that it is very rare. But second night take-overs happen.

56

The subsidized Co's think understudying is an important part of their actors' development, (and so it can be). You may get the original director popping in to understudy rehearsals; though pressure of work often results in less understudy rehearsal than in commercial theatre where things are done more according to the letter of the law. There, understudies are called regularly to rehearse with the stage-management in command. For a commercial manager the need for understudies is an irritating expense. He will try and fulfil it as cheaply as possible. You may be asked to cover five parts, or all of your gender. Once this happened and *two* male principals were 'off' the same night. An actor relaxing in a pub found himself thrust on with the book. In the West End this is not good public relations.

Understudying is often a thankless task. You must be in the theatre all the time your principal is performing (though arrangements are sometimes made with stage management for you to sit in pubs or even at the end of telephones). It's a jittery existence because really you want to play the part. You can't play it like *her* but you have worked hard on it. You know it, you've thought of little moments to make your own, and yet it seems never will you get the chance. She's as strong as a horse, and that cough you heard echoing down the corridor the other afternoon was simply a matinée tickle (it disappears at sunset). But she may trip in that long dress. Have you considered drugging her tea?

If your only function is to understudy, then at least you are getting paid, you are involved with a Group, you can see the play whenever you want, and you will get to know it very well. You may be able to take your knowledge of the production and your role(s) and purvey them elsewhere. First-hand acquaintance with London productions is sought in other market-places.

Stage Management

The actor is not the only person who is involved in a successful performance. Stage-management (let's put scene-shifters, fly-men, electricians, board operators, assistant stage-managers, deputy stage-managers, company stage-managers, under the heading)—all of them actively contribute to what happens during a performance. Some actors have stage-management experience and some don't. Those who do understand the theatrical process better than those who don't, but may not make better actors.

Theatre's a team game and no team plays well that does not respect the territory of each individual. X must do his job and Y hers. No actor gives the performance of which he's capable if the vital dagger is missing. No stage-manager gives the vital lighting cue if an actor cuts the preceding speech. The performance will be flawed (though these things overcome; an experienced company manager will have set a dagger permanently in a drawer to solve such a dilemma, and the stage manager will give the essential lighting cue anyway because she does not depend upon the foibles of actors to make the technical side of the show work). We interdepend; though we put our own work first.

The actor inherits a suspicion that stage-management is an extension of his employer, an arm, as it were, of 'the law' which watches as he works. Stage-management call rehearsal times. They tell you when you have a wig fitting, a publicity photograph. They enter in their prompt copy all moves and all changes of direction, all 'business' and all changes of text. They allocate dressing rooms, they call you on stage, they pay you on Fridays, they harangue you if you're late. They have to enter comments on the show after every performance. If you're drunk it goes in the book.

In our job, as in every other, the only way to work well is with tolerance, with flexibility, with good humour. Fledgeling stage-managers (as well as actors) please note!

C.S.M's.

Company stage-managers do represent the management in the administration of all that takes place on the stage. They are technical chiefs and sometimes oscillate between serving the interests of director and those of employer (for every crea-

58

tive idea is also a monetary one—only thought is free in our business). During performances the C.S.M. can be 'behind' or 'in front' (backstage or in the auditorium), depending upon the technical requirements of the piece and the resulting opportunities to watch the show. It is the job of the C.S.M. to keep the show as the director wishes it.

.S.M's.

Deputy stage-managers run the show from the prompt corner. They are 'on the book' (and have been from the beginning of rehearsals), they know the show thoroughly. Every cue from start to finish is given by them. Actors, stage staff, 'lights' and 'sound' hang on their little green cue lights. In the prompt corner is a switchboard, a microphone, a reading lamp and 'the book'.

A show which ran for six years with a cast of four was so deeply impregnated into the subconscious of all concerned that once when an actor 'dried' at a matinée there was no 'book' from which to prompt him (the stage-manager ran the show from memory). Impasse. They brought the curtain down, started again from the beginning and this time memory came to the rescue at the crucial moment.

Prompting

Prompting is a horrid business, for stage-manager, for actor and for audience. Audiences should remain unaware that anything has gone wrong. The stage fiction is broken if they see and hear the hiatus. Best is for the actor to get himself out of the difficulty, by 'knitting' (making words up) to bridge the gap. Actors can also make noises instead of words for a few seconds. The audience usually imagines they didn't catch that bit and wishes you'd speak up! (This device works best in verse plays because metrical rhythm allows for audio-suggestion). Next best is for a prompt to be given so tactfully that the audience's ignorance is bliss. We have an advantage over audiences. They don't know what should happen next. It has been known for an actor to stroll to the prompt corner, refurbish his memory

59

and take up the thread from where he left off (the audience unaware of the disaster).

It is dangerous for one actor to prompt or help another over lines (though I was helped on my first professional appearance this way. I was far too excited to remember my lines!) It depends upon the text of the piece of course; chat *au naturel* is easy to play about with, but a more formal text (Shaw, Miller, verse of course) is a different thing entirely. Mrs Siddons could make up blank verse (at an Inn she said '*You've brought me Porter, boy, I asked for Ale*') but most of us can't, impromptu. If you help someone who has dried it looks as though it's you who's in trouble: you're the one seen making it up.

'Drying'

An American star of the '30's dried after making a grand entrance through upstage centre-doors. She simply turned her back to the audience and addressed the maid: 'What was the message Clara?'

But the late Robert Atkins is said to have used his understudy in an original way. Atkins was Enobarbus in *Antony and Cleopatra* and his understudy was his page. (Shakespeare allows for no such attendant). One night, in a famous passage, Robert Atkins dried: it was the description of the first meeting of Antony and Cleopatra. He turned to his page/understudy and said 'Philomel, tell thou the tale'.

You can dry in different degrees. Sometimes it is a dreadful shock to the nervous system, you go blank, deaf, you can't hear what's being whispered at you. It is remarkable what audiences don't notice. We exaggerate everything that happens during a performance. We are in a heightened state.

Professionals know their lines, they don't hope they will. Often you will think you don't know what to say next but words will come when they're needed. Don't think ahead, that's the worst cause of anxiety. Be in the moment, listening. If you tell yourself you'll dry, answer yourself that you won't. If you can relax and trust that the words will come, nine times out of ten they will. On the tenth occasion you will have to take a prompt as every actor has to. It doesn't matter. World famous musicians 'dry'. How are they prompted?

Front-of-House (F.O.H.) is that part of the theatre devoted to our patrons. Architects think this is the most important part of the building. This is where comfort and attractive design and space and lavatories are (things like that!) We've always had to beat the drum: 'Roll up, roll up. Our theatre's bright and lively. There's a lot going on (not just plays). Coffee bars, crêches, piano recitals, film shows, a restaurant with ambition. Folk guitars at a late hour. Something for everyone. You must be pretty dull if you can't find *any* of our offerings palatable.'

The front-of-house is the shop window. People must stop and look and be aware that they have a theatre, their local.

The box-office at the front is more important than the stage-door keeper at the back. You can't dispense with box-offices (unless we reach a time of free-for-all ha! ha!, and then people will have to be educated to take an interest in what they haven't paid for!). The box-office is a confined space in which to do vital work. Go into one, work in one, you won't quickly complain about their sullenness again. Much book-keeping goes on there, continual checking and counter checking—of seating plans or books of tickets or both and cash against stubs, and the advance in the Long Tom and agency seats and percentages. Producers, C.S.M's or Theatre managers or even, perhaps, 'stars' and backers who have an interest in box-office activity can walk in. Every night balances are drawn up, cash lodged in deposit accounts, returns made to the front-of-house manager. It isn't surprising that box-office personnel aren't always the most charming 'phone talkers in the world.

They should be. They should ooze charm and inveigle all callers (invisible or real) into the theatre. They should be as seductive as Mephistopeles. They should charm rude and indecisive patrons into commitment and contentment. They should be a Venus fly-trap; but they're human.

They don't answer 'phones with a success on their hands. They go at a pace that suits them. If people are rude they are rude back. They make mistakes. They get irritable.

Nevertheless a first-class box-office staff can work wonders for us all.

House Manager

The house manager isn't just a smart man in a dinner jacket, a symbol of luxury who, if the mood takes him, smiles at the customers and lends an air of high-life to the place. He is boss of the front. He's in charge of ushers and usherettes. He receives nightly box-office returns (and passes them on to all concerned). He represents the management to the audience. He smooths the upset of double-booking or someone fainting. He has the invidious job of telling audiences of cast changes or strikes by stage staff. He announces that there's a bomb in the theatre. He locks up last, leaving the building to the charge of the night-watchman.

Ushers and usherettes sometimes make a row by coming into the auditorium just before curtain time (act or end) and noisily pulling exit drapes establishing their serving positions. They spoil concentration for audience and actor, often at a crucial moment in the play (near the curtain-line). In a run they get into the habit of being there on the dot and are oblivious of the play's effect.

Front-of-house managers should insist on sensitivity from their staff.

Critics

Critics are paid for appraising our work. The word *critic* comes from the Greek word for *judge*. Nobody likes being judged and being a judge cannot be a bowl of roses.

By 'the critics' we mean those men and women who write about what we do in the newspaper. There are the 'dailies' with their large circulation and quick impact, 'Sundays' with their fashionable readership and considered lengthy notices, and there are monthly, quarterly and annual publications. There is also radio and television: critics are heard on both.

Critics are very often creative people, who are good at articulating what they feel and think about what they hear, see or read. They may have special knowledge of their subject although they may not have practised it. They may be journalists (good writers), or reporters (newspapermen bringing back the news). Sometimes sports reporters cover Racine: they are not pleased and nor are we.

Critics link Theatre to society. In the provinces one man may be responsible for writing about all Theatre in the area. He has an important influence on the community—and on us. He can help us greatly if he cares to. So can all critics. Enthusiasm is their saving grace! Kenneth Tynan was an entertaining critic: his 'judgments' showed through his prose: he didn't pronounce verdicts.

In America now one man has the power to make or break a show. This is unhealthy, and most unfortunate for theatre-people. Critics should not control what the public does or does not see, they are not censors. How can one man's opinion always be 'right'? What is 'right' as regards criticism?

Critics are necessary. They lead public opinion about Theatre. In the early '6o's they were crucial in the establishment of the Royal Shakespeare Company and this led to the National Theatre Company being set up. They tell us when we seem relevant to things (Arthur Miller says good plays catch something that's 'in the air'). They're an antidote to theatric self-love and the spirit of incest that hovers around productions. They cool our burning aspirations and tell the world when we've struck gold. They have a splendid tradition behind them, from Longinus to—? It would be invidious to single out a member of the current cast.

The habit of describing performances (and those of individual actors) seems to have caught on in the eighteenth-century with writers like Hazlitt and Lamb. It continued throughout the nineteenth-century and is now, on the whole, reduced to short summaries in newspapers. But critics do more than simply report events.

The nature and function of Drama has long intrigued inquiring minds, and people who contribute to Theatre often write about it too. Literary creators think that words can pin down anything, and for philosophers there has been a rich mine of musing in Theatre; mask and face, the real and the unreal, epiphanies and so on. Critics also educate: they herald new theatrical forces (like Archer and Shaw did Ibsen) and they explain to a puzzled public what the avant-garde is doing. Critics have themselves been important dramatists; but creation and criticism may war against each other.

Critics are not typical of any audience, and they see too much to understand the tastes of those who come infrequently. They live in the element of Theatre and cannot imagine the many and mundane reasons why people come to a particular theatre on a particular night. Their standards become exclusive, and their sense of proportion about what might or might not be 'caviare to the general' (for after all our wider purpose is always to reach more people) is under constant strain. Their own capacity for enjoyment is severely taxed, going, as they do, most nights of the week, to see something, somewhere.

The life of a critic seems attractive (it seems to consist of going free to all kinds of entertainment, travelling too, telling of Asia in Slough, and having 'expenses'!) But there are snags: like many a tedious evening, rushing your copy in, not getting facts wrong (or suffering storms of protest) and being able to comprehend everything that is set before you. A critic who was leaving the English première of *Waiting for Godot* at the interval was told to keep his seat by a literary agent. 'The play is significant' he was told.

For actors, critics take the place of Mother (will she, won't she approve?). But it's important not to act for anyone but your fellow actors. How can you act for the critics? You're always in a play, doing something in a play, not standing there showing your smirky self off.

Notices affect us. It is best not to read them. It is only our lust for praise that makes us do so. Usually we regret it. We may be depressed by things said and adversely affect the show. Or we may be flattered and further dig that pit of self-esteem which is bottomless.

We should, while playing, ignore the comments of critics, but we should, as actors, be glad that intelligent and caring minds do 'criticize' our work. Imagine a world without criticism! We would only have the sounding board of some applause to reward us, like one hand clapping.

Praise of actors is not the first duty of critics (nor praise of anyone necessarily). You may be championed but you may be disowned. You may be 'discovered', or you may, with any luck, work well and regularly without the searchlight catching you. Critics and actors must co-exist and only occasionally open fire upon each other. One of our most extraordinary actors was panned in leading roles in two successive productions. 'Grumble, grumble, grumble' he said, 'you don't know what to do for the best.' Keep going, from strength to strength, like him!

Flops

In Moscow there is a corner of the Stanislavsky museum that is preserved in memory of his artistic failures. Every artist has the right to fail. We have to expose our failures (and directors too). Writers, painters, composers don't. We are paid to do a job: we cannot do it in our own time, we cannot postpone the day of opening.

Theatre costs a lot of money to produce (as we are all now aware). The professional actor has to succeed on a professional level, and this may inhibit him from developing his powers to their full extent and daring either to be very good or very bad.

Acting's a job (my title is no doubt conceived because of such pressures). In England we have never been able to take Theatre seriously as art. That is why no-one knows whether it is one or not. In America they have carried on—in dedicated

Groups—the work and example of Russia's whole-hearted commitment to the possibilities of Theatre. And this has produced both good and bad results. The danger of over-dedication (if there is such a thing) is that our work becomes divorced from life and may be no more than a manifestation of Group neuroses.

'The actors work on himself' can be done—given a strong will and desire—in isolation, and so the practice of daily limberings of voice and body and the disciplines of mind that creating characters demands, is left to the individual. The need that actors have for serious thinking and serious work is seen in the way many despise commercial opportunities, preferring to get little or no pay and do work that is meaningful to them. When acting is an art it has the quality of redemption which is of more value than money.

The more 'experimental' Theatre that's brewing the better. Anything is worth trying (so long as much money is not involved). On the shop floor of Theatre the sky's the limit. 'Ah! but a man's reach should exceed his grasp/or what's a heaven for?' exclaims Robert Browning in *Andrea del Sarto*. We act, a lot of us, to exceed our grasp, and if you aim high it is inevitable that sometime you will come crashing down. If you attempt parts you're not ready for, if demands are made on you you cannot meet, if your desire exceeds your technical resources, you'll come a cropper. But to have the chance! and maybe— to levitate!

If you are prominent in a failure you will be heart-broken and probably paranoid. Yet what is success?

It may be that you personally have succeeded, done all that could be asked, achieved things you haven't before.

The public stayed away. The critics universally agreed it was not as it should be. Somehow the production never caught fire, it's hard to say why. No it wasn't your fault, it was . . .

It may take a time to put a flop behind you, and it may take employers a long time to disassociate you from a flop. Think long into the future, and if you can, like having had a horse-fall, get on again quick.

4 The media

Radio—that world seemingly so tucked away from where the action is—is a rewarding field of employment for actors. Rewarding in all senses of the word. A high proportion of good and interesting work is done, the hours are civilized, the company often so too.

Radio

The results can be exciting. Many listeners think radio drama the best in the world.

Two prize-winning students—a male and a female—have the chance to go into radio direct from their Drama School. The remainder must gather one year's professional experience before writing to the Drama Department, BBC. You will be sent an application form and, depending on how your answers are received, you will be asked to audition. If you do, you'll spend some time in a studio with a director and an engineer to yourself. You have to go through your paces. Give them as wide a variety of vocal entertainment as you can (animals and babies not excluded). Your tape is then stored and producers (they're directors too in *Sound*) can listen at their leisure. Do they?

You have to be a good sight reader to work in Radio, and very adept at turning the pages of scripts. Work is done fast. You must be a quick thinker and able to 'lift' a part off the page, bring it alive without props, costume etc., indeed without moving from the spot (though actors get into unbelievable contortions trying to contain their feelings and the nervous energy they generate).

Radio is the most intimate form of communication that we have. Mind speaks to mind, nothing to distract. Radio acting is always mentally demanding, the utmost concentration is required. Thought has to be quite specific, every thought. Vocally you must demand attention from listeners, most of whom are not sitting quietly listening.

The best plays deserve proper attention. Stereophony has increased listening pleasure, but the encirclement of Quadrophony is more dubious. The idea is to make the listener a

Radio acting

participant, like Theatre sometimes 'involves' the audience. How many enjoy this experience?

Technique

The 'technique' of radio acting may be picked up in a morning. In mono, the 'mike' is 'alive' on both sides, therefore people can speak to it from either side. If you play a two-handed scene you will face each other *but you speak to the 'mike', not the other person*. The microphone receives your performance. Whatever you do and wherever you do it from it is for the benefit of the microphone. You learn that if you speak into it from the sides the sound is deadened, made distant; and if you speak from too far away aural imbalance will result. You soon get used to the right distances.

In Stereophony the microphone is sensitive to what is going on at the sides too. You must be more careful about taking exact positions than with mono. In Quadrophony the central mike(s) is alive all the way round.

Drama Rep.

At Broadcasting House (B.H.) there is a Drama Repertory Company. Twenty-two men and eight women are engaged on six-monthly contracts. You can be given three of these before doing something else. The Rep. are paid a basic weekly wage and programmes which are repeated or sold bring in more cash permutated on it. In the Rep. you are booked by producers like taxis. You may complain if you want to.

Producers vary from the excellent and exciting to the dull and over-literary. It is not necessary in radio for that chemistry to happen between actors, or between director and actor that is the stuff of Theatre. Radio may not be your medium. Great patience is needed and being cooped-up can be trying. Silence is the basic requirement in a studio (though there's an ante-room where you can let off some steam).

BBC

Commercial radio stations have found that Drama is too expensive for them to undertake. The BBC have fifty years of plays behind them: they have the facilities and the expertise.

69

They have a tradition which has produced some of the finest writing of the century (Dylan Thomas, Louis MacNeice, Henry Reed, Giles Cooper, Frederick Bradnum). The list could go on long. Radio is the prime guardian of the English language. Economies must not impoverish its example.

At Bush House (in the Aldwych, on the Strand) the BBC broadcasts overseas. Drama is produced for this market, though it is geared to listeners for whom English is a second language.

At Kensington House (in Shepherd's Bush) experimental programmes are made. Here too, is the best radio canteen.

Across the road from B.H. is a Schools' Rep. of four men and one woman. They are responsible for the drama that goes out in the weekly thirteen hours of programmes during term-time.

Free-lance performers are used by the BBC in all departments. Any actor may be employed. Famous names and faces are to be seen at the 'Beeb', though some of the most creative people (the producers, the writers) you won't recognize.

TV Audition

Let's talk of Television. Having a union card, you may ask the BBC casting director for a camera audition.

You'll have an interview first. You'll be asked about yourself and you'll fix an audition time.

You'll be told to do three shortish pieces (and you'll bear in mind that they should be contrasting and *parts that you might play on television* (i.e. parts about your own age).

In a small studio you'll do your stuff. You won't be told any particular television tricks. You'll swan in, be given a chair or a table (if you need them), and as you perform a camera standing in front of you will take a picture. What it sees is shown on some monitor screens in the viewing-room. Your audition will not be kept on video-tape. The purpose of it is to let the casting directress see you 'on the box'. She makes notes about you and these are available if anyone enquires after you. From time to time she is able to start people in TV but it is very much harder to get a first job at the BBC than with the Independent Companies.

70

Your television audition will feel an odd affair, especially if you haven't been in front of a camera before. You have to imagine the other person(s) in the scene with you (as in a stage audition), but you must act far more intimately than you would in a theatre. The camera watches your face all the time. You can 'behave' more indulgently than in a theatre. Your face and what's going on in it (through the words) is all you have to offer.

Casting

The Independent Companies do not hold camera auditions. ATV, London Weekend, Thames, and Yorkshire Television boast casting directors (several). These people have considerable influence over our fate. Nothing's logical about our work and which actor finally ends up with which part is very often a tale too tall for belief. The whim of an office secretary can count: but that's the world—it has people in it, we are not masters of our own fortunes. Still, we must proceed as though there were order about, and certainly casting directors take their job very seriously. They work closely with producers and directors. They offer names to those who make the final decision. In casting any part those responsible make out a first eleven (as it were), and a second and a third etc., etc. Everyone wants Laurence Olivier but he's rarely free—thus, you might get the part instead.

When you get a part never make it your business to find out why or how. Assume you are first choice. You might be.

Rehearsals

When you attend your first television rehearsal you'll be surprised at the speed things happen. You'll have been used to Theatre and its ways—a slow, careful approach (comparatively), a long period of rehearsals (hopefully), time for a part to gestate. Television can be like that, it can be thorough (depending on your own working processes), but of necessity it's speeded up considerably. The aim of a TV director is to bring the play to the boil for the one or two days in the studio, when the 'performance' happens. It's like bringing a boat race crew to their peak the day of the race—different from the building of a stage production which must last a long time.

The rhythm is different from Theatre, even from the first reading. The average TV play is done in a more clinical way than for the stage. Don't imagine that you're joining as close-knit a group as you would be for a stage play. TV is a ten to six job. You may think it unexciting.

After the first reading of a TV play (those round the table mutters where people gaze stiffly at the pages before them seeing no words except their own, and those through a feverish brain); Make-up and Wardrobe are at hand in the persons of often personable ladies who have usually thought about the character and have ideas about how he/she should look. They may have agreed things with the director or at least referred to him. Often this is the first stage in a tactful battle which may last until the very moment you're committing your performance to tape. You may have thought long and hard about your character. What you wanted to look like may not tally with what other people have thought. How tactful are you? How winning? What *should* happen is that you put your case to the director (you must have his say-so about appearance). He may say leave it for a bit, see what rehearsals produce in new ways of thinking of the part. He's got to keep everyone happy. Take deep breaths. Take the wardrobe lady out for a drink, take the make-up lady to the cinema, bide your time, erode their resistance (everyone likes being creative, making contributions—especially to your part!). *You may change your mind. Don't stiffen with pride about things creative. The imagination works in funny ways. Remain open-minded until you know what's best. Then you must try to achieve what you want. But ours is group work. The world has people in it.*

Professional Approach

Actors vary in the way they approach their work. Perhaps it changes from part to part, from group to group, from director to director. Professionalism consists first of effort, of not being lazy, of taking your work seriously. You shouldn't turn up at a first rehearsal without having read the script. This is not to say

72

that someone who turns up totally unprepared will not give a fine performance, a better performance than you perhaps; but there is everything to be said for a *professional* attitude, for contributing to the areas in which we should contribute, for throwing ideas into the melting pot of the rehearsal-room, for *taking your work as seriously as it deserves*. And there's the rub of course! The quality of the plays we do varies in every degree and in every medium. Sometimes it is hard to respect the material, (and yet we always have to respect ourselves, at least the way in which we do the job, otherwise we are close to being the flotsam and jetsam that people sometimes accuse us of being). Look how hard Morecambe and Wise work. Ken Dodd has 'I must rehearse, I must rehearse' built into his patter! Most leading actors (in all mediums) work extremely hard. They give much time and thought to what they do. That is why they are leaders. By caring you can make work meaningful.

The rehearsal period must be fruitful, though you will sometimes feel that a small part has nothing to it. It may not have. You are earning your living. Other people do unrewarding work. Some work will only yield what it will yield. Other areas of your life have to compensate for what work does not provide. Acting can fulfil a great many needs—perhaps that's why we turn to it in the first place—but we are not stretched all the time. Sometimes we are bored to death. We're often temperamentally lazy people (have you read the charming essay by J. B. Priestley 'On Doing Nothing'?) though no-one works harder when they must. But it is disappointing when work provides only acquaintanceship and cash.

Group Needs

There is something labelled a 'hierarchy of human needs'. It starts with basic things like food and shelter, and once those are satisfied we need other human beings, 'society'. Then we like to make our impact on the Group (the ego needs expression), and when we feel important we like to think we're living to some purpose (spiritual needs, God, etc.).

I wish more directors understood that people have a right

(and a real need) to be part of a group, to contribute when they can or feel they can. Commercial pressures and 'success' take over from people as being our professional focus of attention.

Art may be long and life short, but the irony is that art suggests values which lovers of art and fewer 'artists' can live up to. Drama finally preaches the great human virtues—compassion, understanding, generosity etc. And yet the way in which our work is sometimes achieved is the opposite. However, contradiction is at the root of existence. The most delightful people may produce dreary work.

TV Direction

Certain TV directors work out a camera script (what the viewer will see) before rehearsals begin (just as some directors have moves worked out at a first theatre rehearsal). But directors in either medium who rigidly maintain these positions from first to last are repressive.

Some TV shows are technical nightmares, but it is the mark of a very insecure person to think rigidly where group creativity is concerned. It means that nothing is quite as good as it could be. For an actor to be told where to go before he opens his mouth to speak, before he has played the scene with his colleagues, before they have mined it for whatever gold it will yield, is not creativity—it is the opposite. There is a breed of TV director who has grown up in the medium and knows nothing of actors and Theatre. His picture is all that concerns him. He doesn't see that what is filling the picture (hearts, minds, faces, emotion, the ingredients of the brew *before* it is photographed) is what counts.

Technique

Television is the most technical medium. It is a mating of film and stage, neither the one nor the other. Rehearsals proceed as though for weekly Rep. and yet all is done for an unseen camera. Directors click their fingers at you, indicating camera cuts, as you try to concentrate on performing. Scenes are short (usually). You have to be pitched just right, to begin, and then

74

to begin again, and again. Television demands a ferocious truth from an actor. A lot of television acting is behaving. A feature film is larger than life, a radio 'mike' wants your thoughts, the stage is there to expand upon, but television is condensed truth. Truth in a corner of a living-room.

Who do you want in your living-room? Cliff Michelmore is affable enough, Ludovic Kennedy relaxed enough, Benny Hill cheerful enough. But which actors (or characters) do you want? They are the successful creatures of TV.

No matter how talented you are television tames you. The power of a Peter O'Toole or an Olivier is not contained by the small screen. It may not be to your discredit if television eludes you. But it will be to the detriment of your earning power! Most actors come to terms with television—if they're given the chance.

You may not have practised television acting at Drama School. Equipment is too costly (even mock-up studios are beyond the resources of most schools), and professional studios are too busy. More camera training must come about, but at the moment only about half-a-dozen schools (in Scotland and London) do any at all. Check brochures when seeking pupillage, and beware ersatz film or television schools. So many are valueless (as are the bubble drama courses advertized from time to time, especially in the summer when innocent foreigners invade. Weekend seminars, amateur-minded wonder schools!— crash courses are usually crass courses. They fill in time. They may be jolly, but their influence is not long-lasting. Theatre professionals are in it for life).

Because of the jerky rhythm of events television acting is most demanding of an actor's technique. Perhaps this is the chief reason for not dwelling on it at schools. A beginner (a student) will have quite enough to worry about, without trying to overcome the vagaries of television drill. Not until you are reasonably experienced can you hope to have the confidence and *discipline* which enables you to start a scene many times at the right pitch, and to stop immediately for any technical reason;

to play tiny takes judging their effect, their impact on the whole, to a nicety.

Cameras are moved from set to set; there are continual retakes for a variety of reasons (so many people are involved in making the thing work). There are 'cheated' shots (where actors have to make artificial moves in order to facilitate camera movement). There are pauses when scenery has to be struck (taken away) to get a shot from a certain angle. 'Prefilming' (exterior location work) has to be run into what's going on in the studio, and at the end of the day there may be 'stills' of a hand (yours?) holding a photograph or the open page of a diary.

Throughout all this the actor gives his performance. He has to be able to switch himself on and off like a tap, or else contain his feelings and thoughts (his 'character') within him—through tea-breaks, technical difficulties, the general paraphernalia that is Television.

That is a description of the real thing and not found at any Drama School: there TV training is only an approximation; but it allows the student to catch a little of the atmosphere, not to think the camera a rude intruder, to understand the drill.

Television acting demands different ingredients from the Stage. You play off yourself more. You use 'yourself', warm the camera with your own personality. But not everybody can do everything.

Professional actors would benefit from somewhere to practise 'telly' before taking a late plunge. Could the TV Companies set up a training place (for technicians and directors too?) Might it be built from money that would otherwise be tax? An experimental house for new ideas new concepts in TV?

Many experienced TV actors profess not to know what the cameras are doing, nor do they want to. They want simply to perform and be oblivious of anything 'technical', anything which will distract from their concentration or characterization.

Some do the opposite, and work very consciously *in terms of the medium* and what it can do: what it can do for us, and what we can do for it. Your working relationship with the director is of paramount importance to what can be achieved in this way.

This is linked to the whole idea of the actor being 'passive', simply serving in his role as best he knows how, or 'active' in the sense that he is a person, a social person, working in conjunction with others to achieve something 'made' by everyone. Acting's a job. You play a part and you play the play. What we do (directors and cameramen too) is measured by it's effect on those who watch it. Effect does not necessarily mean 'trick', it does not pre-suppose 'lies'. It supposes a mind, it supposes 'art', something consciously made.

No matter how marvellously you perform only the cameras will make it meaningful. You have to be flexible and accommodate the cameras. Sometimes you have to compromise for them.

Producer's Run

You've had two weeks' rehearsal for an hour's play. Towards the end of the second week the rehearsal room will be visited by the producer and his staff and a representative selection of technicians who are working on the show. They will know the script and will no doubt have had meetings with the director, agreeing on what can or can't be done. But this is the first time they've seen the piece in action. Atmosphere in the rehearsal room grows more tense that day. This is your first audience (and will be your last): that's what's so unnerving about people closely watching shows arranged for television. The director has thought how best it should be done in terms of cameras, machines that can capture nose flickers or make the angle of an ear most significant, and there you are faced (positively crowded out) by real live people, and people who are hard to impress, (they've become immune to a great deal of what plays and actors can do!) It requires great self-control to do what the director expects you to do: part of oneself wants to 'entertain the folks'! This tug is felt most keenly in light entertainment shows, when after rehearsing for cameras, a pack of people is let in to gaze and roar upon you. You are confused. Who is your performance for? To whom are you offering it? The cameras.

Actors have to be sly ones sometimes. Quick, cool thinkers, like good centre-forwards in front of goal.

Rehearsal Room

Television rehearsal rooms are functional places. They have little atmosphere, little warmth. They are big (studios are bigger). They look more like gymnasiums than anything else: of course they do have dancers in them as well as thespians. At the 'Acton Hilton', the BBC tower block provides antiseptic green rooms on all floors. The canteen is at the top and, if it's nice, you can sit on a verandah and gaze over Hanwell, Brentford and the M4.

The lack of a place to go when you are not needed for work is felt keenly at Elstree (ATV). It's a frightful imposition to spend one's day silently and without distracting from whatever work is going on. Sometimes in rehearsal for a stage piece, group concentration is helpful. It provides an audience when audiences are the purpose of the work. But there are good reasons why actors should not feel bound by the atmosphere engendered in the corner of a large room. Your scene might have a different flavour from the other. It may be unhelpful to 'catch' the mood and tensions of other scenes and performances.

Time is a vital consideration of the Independent Companies. Their income is derived from advertizers. Nothing can cut into the 'commercials'. Scripts are always treated with this in mind. Sometimes actors lose their favourite scenes.

Studio Days

When your first studio day arrives (not more than half an hour's studio material can be recorded in any one day), you will be given a make-up call by the assistant floor-manager. You must not be late. There are two Gods in the profession—Dionysus (the Greek God who started it all) and *Punctuality*. These days you are fortunate to work—to work and be late is suicidal. Get into your costume before you report to make-up. It should be waiting for you in your dressing-room. You might also find a dresser there. This dresser may be pleasant/unpleasant and useful/useless. Some don't know a 'stock' from a 'bustle' or a pair of spats from a chinchilla wrap. Some are temporaries. All will give you their christian names. If your dresser is useful (sometimes you depend on them for quick changes) tip him/her. There's a vague rule that tipping should take place (it's an item allowed for on your professional allowances at income tax time), but lately, with the levelling of social classes and all that, and the decline in the standards of dressers (yes), the transaction may prove embarrassing. If you do tip, mean it.

Dressed, you will go to 'make-up', a mirrored room, stiff with the scent of Max Factor and pink with the shifts of the girls. It's a nice place before the action begins. Relax, the problems are in their hands. Your theatre training will incline you to take an active part in what is done to you, and certainly you should look as you wish, but television requires subtler blends than the stage, and colour TV brings its own problems. The make-up girl does her best for you (and herself!). One of them will be around the studio floor to keep your appearance as it should be; and to dab you with a cologned chamois leather if you sweat. The lights are hot you see.

Waiting

Now you are ready to rehearse—but you won't be needed. All calls are early (time is money), and people who put on shows (in all media) work more slowly than they say they will.

Waiting is what an actor does a good deal of in his working life. If you are not a patient person you will become one. Films are where you wait longest (it may take a morning to erect the set and lights for a shot), but in television you wait too. Your fee covers your waiting. It's a problem, sometimes excruciating. Whenever we are called we must do our job—act. Inside you is a piece of clockwork that is your performance and you may be told to *go* any time; whatever you've been thinking, whether you're tired or not, whether you've just eaten or are hungry. Only you can prepare yourself, sort out how you can be in the frame of mind you should be in when you're told to *go*. *Do not waste energy at work. You are not there primarily to amuse yourself!*

Keep highly informed about what's going on: you may be able to gauge when you'll be wanted. Experience will tell you what the problems are that have to be sorted out before they get to you. Experience will tell you when you can have a drink and when you shouldn't, and when not to get involved in a political argument because you'll need all your energy within five minutes *for work*. Waiting, waiting to act—sometimes it can seem as long as Vladimir and Estragon wait for Godot.

Newspapers, novels, writing pads, decks of cards, pocket chess, travel scrabble, 'Botticelli', actors need all these to stave off ennui. Actors are the most accomplished crossword addicts. May I mention a game you may not know? We call it *Word-square*. Rule sixteen small boxes onto a piece of paper, thus:

	B	A	T	H
ENGLISH ARISTOCRACY	BEDFORD	ARUNDEL	THOMAS MOWBRAY	HANOVER
COUNTRIES	BELGIUM	ALASKA	TRINIDAD	HAITI
CLASSICAL COMPOSERS	BRUCH	THOMAS ARNE	TALLIS	ENGELBERT HUMPERDINCK
FILM STARS (Female)	BARBRA STREISAND	ANNE TODD	TALLULAH BANKHEAD	JEAN HARLOW

Take turns to pick subjects and write them down on the left. Then choose a four letter word to go across the top. Get it?

You can award points according to the number of players. If four play award four points for a correct answer that no-one else has, and so on, down to one point if all four have the same answer. The winner has the most points.

80

This is an excellent game to suit all capacities. You can make as many boxes as you like (but you'll need a word across the top big enough to cover every column).

You're on. You're wanted for camera rehearsal. . . .

he Studio

You walk through the heavy door with the red light that goes on when *recording* commences. The huge studio will be divided up into sets for the different scenes to be played in. Way above, suspended from the grid are a hundred lamps. They cover the whole space, allowing light to be placed where it's needed. The cameras are ranged round the acting area, you'll recognize it from what went on in rehearsal; but now furniture will be the genuine article, props will be 'practical'; the blue-print of the rehearsal room where anything serves as anything else, (a folding chair for a Queen Anne, a piece of tape for a mantel-shelf) has come to precise life. You take your place, outside a 'real' door, waiting to enter on cue. Stop! Your cue was a visual one (when Mother walked towards the window). You can't see her! No problem. The Floor-Manager will wave his hand.

The Floor Manager controls the studio floor. He wears headphones through which instructions come from the director. He conducts the day and the 'take' on the morrow. He waves his hand, you enter. Stop! Camera No. 2 (it's got its number for all to see) has difficulty in manoeuvring around a pillar to get the shot of your entrance. Try it again.

The camera is still late to see the door opening. Never mind says the director, go on, it'll come with practice.

There may be four cameras to shoot this scene. The one with the red light on it (lit) is the one whose picture the viewers will see. Other cameras may be photographing alternative shots, but up in the control room (where the director is) just one picture is being selected at any given time by the Vision Mixer.

Like a 'technical' stage rehearsal, things stop and start all the time. Every problem has to be faced as it arises, and sorted out. When all is smooth, a 'run' will be attempted, and then another, and then—you will be made nearly immortal!

'Live' TV

Ten years ago there was 'live' television. The weekly two-part serials used to be transmitted live, and those who did live shows rightly think themselves warriors of a different sort from today's softies. It may be that lack of money will see the return of live drama to the box: editing time will be saved, so will a lot of extra man hours and machine time.

If live TV drama does come back there must be longer rehearsal time, *longer with the cameras*. The strain, otherwise, can be horrendous. In the theatre a production is rehearsed long enough to allow the structure to take firm shape. It must be so in live TV, otherwise the nerves and neuroses of actors are played on in a cruel way.

Amongst producers and directors there are two schools of thought: those who favour the live atmosphere, insisting that everyone (cameramen, technicians, control room personnel and performers) give of their very best because they have to, and those who see the advantages of carefully made shows (where shots can be taken again and the whole piece edited so that the rhythm of it—the visual rhythm—is most satisfying).

Most actors enjoy the relaxation that 'non-live' performing brings. Less energy is spent on terror and more on concentration. But we are performers, in the instant performing market. We mustn't forget that we're doing our job because we want to expose ourselves (!) If we stop wanting to do that—or are not prepared to do it, we must question our professional motives.

The 'Take'

When TV shows are running smoothly there are broadly two ways in which they can be 'put in the can'. Each scene can be finally rehearsed and then recorded, one by one (though probably not in 'story order' because of the logistics of the studio); or the whole piece can be finally rehearsed, and then 'shot' straight through from beginning to end. Different directors use different methods and their choice depends upon the nature of the piece.

TV can be a wearing process. Final 'takes' are often done at the end of a long day. No wonder the bars of television companies do well! People look forward to their after-show drink.

The Independent Companies pay more than the BBC. A Civil Service mentality pervades the 'Beeb's' approach to money. Over the years your worth will inch up. You are rewarded for endurance!

Minimum current rates for a half-hour's play at the BBC is £66. This is doubled for an hour and trebled for over an hour.

The Independent Companies multiply a basic fee by as many networks as will see the show. There are five networks altogether: London, Midlands, Lancashire, Yorkshire, and 'the rest'.

Within two years of its first showing, a repeat of a programme entitles you to 75 per cent of your fee. After this the percentage increases.

Programmes may be sold to other countries, and what these countries pay for them varies enormously. Rich countries may give you more than your original fee, poor countries far less. But you will benefit, if only by the odd penny (sometimes it costs more to send the fee than it's worth).

'Equity' of course closely negotiates every line of every contract for television. There is nothing haphazard about what you are paid. All new agreements are available for any actor to study.

Every time you do a job, what you are paid is negotiable.

Long-running TV series pose problems. They are hard work (that is to say the regularity of studio days and the learning of lines and not going stale and remaining sociable with people you see daily make heavy demands). What happens is that the actor sinks into his character: it may become his doppelganger. You are either happy to have a fixed identity (the public know exactly who you are) and regular work and marvellous pay, or you're not. There are no rules. The money would tempt a saint, and some actors are not versatile enough to do anything else. Many are able to do much else because they become well-known and rich and want and can afford to do other work (perhaps bring it about).

Some series-regulars have reached an age when settled hours, excellent pay, the warmth of having a respected status in group and community are just what they need. Some may feel that twenty or thirty years slog has brought its reward.

Opening fêtes becomes a bore! What you had for tea yesterday (do you bake your own scones?) and who your friend is and what charities (if any) you support become concerns of national gravity. Both your lives become public. Three nights a week you're the lavatory attendant in the series and the other four you can hardly call your own. You need all the money to achieve privacy—taxis, sudden dashes, escape at any price. You buy a cottage far away from reach and lock yourself in!

But solvency is nice. It's what most people are after. You can afford a family. (You've probably got one anyway). Success! Comfort! Indulgence!

Comes the last episode (for series like *Coronation Street* and *The Archers* which never seem to end are very, very rare) is it possible to save enough to remain rich or comfortable in England now? When you're not paid every Friday?

In some ways the more famous you are (as your character the harder it might be to get new work. Still you've lived a bit, ridden high, made a million friends and admirers. You're an actor aren't you? What did you expect?

It is unwise to be snobbish about the acting of others, wherever it takes place. No-one remains five years in a series (series seem perpetual and are usually original scripts: serials are finite and are usually adaptations) without being able to do your job. And who can tell how clever you are? How unlike yourself? Or how like but how subtly like? Some characterizations on television become legends (The Steptoes, Frank Marker, Alf Garnett). The actor has found a role he was 'born to play': which is probably what most of us are looking for.

84

To a young actor *films* may seem the ultimate goal, for it is only on film that we are transported larger-than-life around the world and may be seen after we are dead. The 'poor player that struts and frets his hour upon the stage and then is heard no more may be heard again. Film is how we know Charles Laughton and Marilyn Monroe and even Sir Johnston Forbes-Robertson. To most of us, films are the big time, to be a film star the dream of childhood. Jean Gabin and Spencer Tracy were my heroes before I'd heard of Laurence Olivier or Ralph Richardson. Now of course, television has stepped in between stage and screen and—created its own legends (Gilbert Harding, *The Avengers, Monty Python*). However, when people are familiar enough to be regularly in your living-room they do not seem as wonderful as seen rarely, blown up big at the Gala. Films are still the big time. They pay more than anywhere else. Film stars are the richest actors (though film stars can be made out of non-actors). Films go for beauty, male and female. Films cast super-images before us and we reach up to them.

It is possible to character-act your way to the Stars, but a great many of us will never be seen in heroic proportions on the silver screen. The present state of the British Film Industry (B.F.I.) suggests that fewer and fewer of us will get the opportunity. Hammer Productions hammer out their silly tales and *Carry on Behind* (or is it 'Up'?) is being made at the moment. The cost of films makes Producers keen to see a return for their money. That's why the horror and 'sexploitation' movies are about the only films to carry on in Britain at the moment. They appeal to a lot of people. So did *The Sound of Music*. Little else seems to.

Traditionally the film business is cumbersome. The size of the screen clearly influences the psychology of those who illuminate it—big budgets, big stars, big bosoms, big cigars: that was Hollywood, the fabrication that spawned myths, and the men and women who made them and were unmade too. With the coming of television, cinema lost its unique appeal. The last twenty years have seen the cinema perform many contortions to keep its audience. It can still do things bigger and better than anywhere else—so long as it has the money. You can't ignore cinema like you can television. Some people dream in cinemascopic-panavision with quadrophonic sound!

Pay

Actors are paid by the day or by the week, whichever is cheaper. It is difficult to name a starting price for film work— £50 a day? £75? A hundred and fifty pounds a week?

Traditionally films pay well, though nowadays, on the bottom rungs, television might equal it. Big stars get colossal amounts—presumably they're worth it in terms of box office receipts; but until super-salaries are trimmed, those underneath are entitled to ask for all they can get.

Film Directors

Directors use film in different ways so there are few constants about what actors are required to do. It's as well to learn lines *before* you get to the studio: sometimes rehearsals are non-existent (except of course for the cameras): relationships between the characters or indeed *characterization* as such may happen despite of rather than because of the director's approach. The actor's work depends on the way the director works (more than in any other of our jobs). In film the director is king (providing he can deal with the Producers breathing down *his* neck). The best film-makers conceive and execute 'their own thing'. It can be disturbing to work with such people for only in their heads is what everyone should be doing. Some are better at communicating with actors than others. Some are martinets.

At the making of *Frenzy* Hitchcock sat before us protesting his boredom. His work had been done ten months before. He had planned the film, frame by frame, and that is what he saw as he sat there. The way we played the scenes was determined by the visual shape Hitchcock had planned before he met any of the actors. He is a darling of Producers because he leaves no wastage on the cutting-room floor. It seems he hardly minds who acts in his films, action and image are nearly all. His camera is always

86

busy, it noses its way around, pushes in to explore. It comes across actors acting and moves on.

Other directors depend very much on their actors generating a life for them to 'shoot'. Ken Russell may demand anything and plenty of it: he gives actors enough scope to dare greatly.

Few films respect words.

The Routine

Work begins early. All exterior shots are subject to the dictates of the weather. The light in the sky rules the fates of hundreds of people. Sensible producers try to have alternative 'wet weather' scenes to shoot indoors.

Film is a language: it has a grammar. One basis of this grammar is the 'master shot'. This is a 'take' that sees an entire scene. Commonly, only after the 'master' is shot are other angles considered—close-ups, mid-shots, reverses (camera looking at the other person in the scene). When editing (cutting all the different shots together to make an interesting and rhythmic whole) the 'master' is always on hand if any moment has not been 'covered'.

A sequence is rehearsed, and when lighting men, cameramen, sound recordist, director are happy about what's happening, the actors go to wardrobe and make-up and wait until they are called onto the 'set'. Meanwhile the 'set' is being dressed, lights 'rigged' and all made ready to 'shoot'. The scene is then done again as though for the 'take'. If all is well a 'take' will be taken! Or you may 'rehearse on film' which is a phrase to put people at their ease but means 'shoot'.

The first 'take' may be fine or you may have to do umpteen. *It isn't only actors who are fallible.* Aeroplanes materialize on the word *Action* (the traditional word spoken by the director to synchronize all activities): their drone ruins the shot. A hair gets caught in the camera gate—a human hair or other flotsam that has no business in the immaculate machine. The light may change during a shot; the local populace might infiltrate (local populaces have scant regard for the business of filming); heaven and earth may combine to stymie the most conscientious crew.

From the actor's point of view *any take* may be used when the film is edited: you have to do your very best every time: have a bash, and another, and another—that's what's satisfying about filming.

You are not obliged to do anything involving undue physical risk when filming. Pressure may be put on you but insist that stuntmen do the dangerous things.

If television is a mechanical medium, film is—whatever the latest electronics can achieve. Film can be more doctored than cats. Sub-plots bite the dust, never to be seen again, leading roles are dubbed, shots are inserted after the unit has packed its bags. The actor can only hope his contribution will be noted.

'Post-Sync'

'Post-synchronizing' is a common film operation. It means dialogue or sound must be synchronized with the picture *after* shooting. Film contracts commit you to a certain amount of 'post-synchronizing' (though it's not always necessary). A 'loop' of film (long or short, but a piece that goes round and round on the projector and thus onto the screen) is shown you. You have to marry the words with your mouth on the screen. The same process is used to dub foreign films into English, and here is another field of employment. Peter Sellers was an expert in this, with his remarkable range of accents. You have to characterize completely, as you would if you were 'animating' the voice of a cartoon character.

Advertizing

There is another way of being filmed—in a *Commercial* (the American word for advertizement). Independent Television Companies pay their way (and make their profit) from those who advertize between and during programmes. Firms wishing to advertize on TV have 'commercials' made for them by advertizing companies. These companies write and plan the Ad. and then engage director, crew and actors to film it. Actors are interviewed and auditioned by the advertizing companies, probably not in the presence of the director. You are gazed at, assessed for the purpose in hand, and maybe asked to 'read'.

You must keep a straight face when the punch-line comes up—'I would *never* be without a pair of *Blank's* knickers!' Much time and thought has gone into the writing of the short scenario. The money that surrounds the whole operation is a mighty sum. The making of advertizements is taken entirely seriously from the birth of the 'idea' to the final highly polished piece of film. If advertizements didn't 'pay' they would not, presumably, be made in the quantity and quality they are.

86 per cent of advertizements on television have been found to be perfectly proper and not guilty of lying, distortion or undue pressurizing of the viewer. Therefore in most cases actors need not fear to take part in corruption. Whether we *should* help to sell products to consumers is another matter (we are, after all, in the habit of purveying 'ideas' rather than commodities); but when you consider how much titillation and cruelty, sensationalism and simple dross we do act in, it hardly behoves us to get on a high horse about advertizing tins of peas or new cars. 'Commercials' are a way of earning money: your skill and talent (perhaps) will be required.

ees   You might get £40 simply to appear in a commercial: a day's hard work. You then get more money (probably a percentage of the £40) every ten times the thing is shown. It is impossible to say how much you might earn altogether, but in my experience it is always far less than you dream of (very few advertizements are shown over a long period of time, and very few actors—like the lady who does the Oxo ads.—get taken up by the nation as a sort of mascot; nor do they want to be: it might put an end to their acting career).

If you were 'featured' in a commercial you might get £100 for the day and repeats based on £75 or some percentage of the £100: it's difficult to understand how the figures are arrived at —that's what agents are for—but the Independent Broadcasting Authority (I.B.A.) keeps a record of all monies due.

It is sometimes possible to do a deal whereby you get a lump sum instead of 'repeats'. You might feel happier about having money in the bank rather than waiting upon the throw of the dice market-wise, (though it would appear to the cynical, or merely realistic, that if a lump sum were offered, more money might be gained from repeat fees!) One thing is certain—it is a waste of time to grieve over not making as much as you hoped you would or as others seem to. Commercials, compared with work sustained over a period of time, are easy money.

'Doing It'

Don't be late the morning of the commercial. No alternative work is possible (as there might be on a feature film). You will be replaced in the twinkling of an eye. The director may have flown in from the States: top directors make commercials all over the world—even those vociferous against Capitalism.

Time is the most precious commodity of the day. Most commercials are made in a day, and everything has to be done before 'wrap-up' time. Work happens at tremendous pressure because the director will want to get a myriad of shots 'in the can' in case his employers or the firm whose product it is want this or that shot, this or that 'angle' (both cinematic and psychological).

You will repeat yourself until you are blue in the face and the heat and lights will wear you into a state of 'zombiehood'. The director will get more tense as time runs out. He'll take it out of someone (you?), as sure as eggs are what we used to go to work on.

The commercial will then be tried out in two different areas of the country and sales compared. If the ad. has had a discernible affect it will be networked, and you will benefit in repeat fees.

You may hope that your best friends don't recognize you: best friends' children, however, are amazingly gifted commercial 'spotters'.

You might well be heavily disguised (physically and vocally) in the commercial—perhaps this should be a consideration of your doing it? But public memory is short. The amount of television put out ensures that oblivion is built-in. Avid viewers see so much they cannot distinctly remember what: it won't be they who call out 'I saw him advertizing underwear' in the middle of your 'To be or not to be'.

Voice-Overs

Voice-overs are a subtler way of earning money. It is said that the voice-over market is monopolized by a handful of speakers, all rich (have you noticed, by the way, how few women's voices are heard as narrators?) Some people do more voice-overs than others (one of them has built a recording studio out of the proceeds): but it is equally true that the advertizing companies are on the listen-out for 'new' voices, voices that will match the product or the image of it, voices that will make a fresh impact on the viewer.

There are *trial* voice-overs. You are paid about half of what you get for the real thing, and the process is to try *you* out and also to try out *their* material. You will probably be told that they will try to use you in the final event, but very often they don't.

Real voice-overs happen when you are shut into a sound-proof booth, with a balloon-shaped 'mike', a clip board with your copy on it and a lot of water. You are something of a prisoner until either your employer (the advertizing company) is satisfied, or studio booking-time runs out.

Outside your commentary booth will be studio technicians (sound experts), and a director (independent of the advertizing firm or part of it); there may be more than one writer (in case a syllable has to be altered) and there may be representatives of the firm whose product you are touting. All these people will have opinions about what you're doing or not doing, or about what you should or should not be doing. The opinions will filter through to you by way of 'feed-back' (when you're not *meant* to have heard the remark), or two-way microphones, when you are.

'Try it again' is the most common piece of direction given.

You try it again.

'Not so— er—have another go.'

You do.

'It was nicer the first time. You're losing warmth.'

In your cell you're beginning to sweat. You give it another whirl.

'Deidre wants to talk to you, listen to Deidre.'

You listen to Deirdre.

'Albert wants to say something.'

Albert says something.

You have another go and this time a frog has jumped into your throat.

Voice-over for an ad .

'Have a drink of water. Relax.'

You wish the water had turned to wine. You take a deep breath.

'In your own time.'

You control your errant diaphragm and read:

Have you ever stopped to think why Blank's fish fingers are the best buy? They're bigger, they're fresher, and they look more like real fingers than other versions of the same thing. Your children will love playing cannibals as they gobble up Blank's bone-building fingers. Two activities for the price of one with Blank's versatile fingers of fish.

'You didn't sound convinced. Have a break. We'll try it again in a minute. The studio's booked till lunchtime isn't it Deirdre?'

You wish it were bedtime.

'We can go on to a fish-finger tea' says Deirdre wittily. 'We'll have to give him another fiver of course.'

'Is that OK actor?'

'Er—perhaps I should ring my agent . . .'

It can get tricky in your booth. Try to think of more amusing things (that shouldn't be difficult). Tell yourself it doesn't matter (which it doesn't much). What can you do except your best? Some sense of dignity must be preserved. Probably, at the end of it all, they'll decide to use the first 'take'.

The person to listen to most is the sound recording engineer. He says practical things because he is the man who controls the quality and volume of what you actually sound like. Do what he tells you.

You are at liberty to get out of your booth and have a quiet word with one of the crowd outside. It sometimes helps to materialize as a person so that you do not remain a disembodied voice which can be abused with impunity.

Many voice-overs are quickly disposed of: I once earned (with repeat fees) £125 in five minutes.

You fit your commentary to a piece of film. You may be cued to speak in at least three ways: by a 'wipe' line which moves vertically across the screen: by a number which is clocked up at the foot of the screen: by the wave of a hand.

Think of a person to speak to in your mind; think of the 'attitude' of the commentary, this will give you the 'tone' of it. As ever, relaxation is the key.

Radio 'Commercials'

Commercial Radio also uses voice-overs, indeed their ads. are only vocal (though music and sound effects play a large part). Voice-overs are done the same way as for 'visuals'. Headphones tell you the 'story' and you add your voice at the right moments.

V.O. fees begin at £20 (though it is difficult to say anything consistent about the current economy). The same wage agreements apply to 'repeats' of V.O.'s that do to 'visuals'.

Commentaries and voice-overs are needed for films made for educational and industrial purposes, as well as commercial ones. Recording companies do anything; from ARGO's Shakespearian canon to E.M.I.'s stories for airflights.

While we're still trapped in front of a microphone a word about *narrations* and *commentaries* that are matched to film.

Microphone Commentaries

There is a basic problem. An actor wants a role to play, an attitude to act; but many commentaries are flat affairs that play a secondary role to the picture.

At the outset few directors seem to know what they want the commentary to sound like, though they have chosen *you* to do it. Somewhere in you is the 'tone' they're looking for. Many directors think only of words as *information*, they forget that every speaking voice has a human personality behind it.

Difficulties may arise through non-existence of technical terms with which to talk to the actor. Documentary directors rarely work with actors. It is we who must adapt, or try to.

Commentaries can be exhausting affairs: concentration is intense and physical movement decidedly limited. There is always a time limit (though no-one speaks of it)—this adds to the pressure. Directors rarely have the nous to give encouragement when they should, where it would benefit them to say 'Yes, that's it! That's what I'm looking for'. They do not realize that actors approach their work very much in the dark, seeking the right tone, the right inflection, the right style, to be a part of the film, to be an intrinsic part.

Sometimes you will be able to help a director with the style of the commentary. We must narrate *positively*, even though it may be impersonally, coolly, unobtrusively.

It is unreasonable to ask an actor to speak a commentary to a film he does not see or hear. His words will be divorced from the rest of the material. 'Wildtrack' commentaries are a waste of time (in my opinion): the actor won't connect with his subject.

'Multi-Media'

'Multi-media' is the name given to 'shows' compiled in a way that uses more than one 'medium'. A good deal of Theatre qualifies for the title, but more and more it is used for commercial and trade purposes. Live sketches, with film: music and closed circuit TV: striptease and lecture: these are the possibilities.

'Sales meetings, Conferences, Dealer meetings, Exhibitions, Permanent Displays, Training Educational Programmes, Information services, Customer relations, Point-of-Sale, Company prestige, Product prestige, or . . . sheer Entertainment'—that's how one 'Multi-media' firm puts it in its brochure (Roundel).

Actors are used in 'multi-media' in many different capacities. They are also used to train businessmen in public speaking and 'outward show'. We who make a study of how others behave pass back our knowledge of the gesture. (Who is the actor, who the 'real person'?)

5 The public

When the public are sitting watching, and we're in our parts, everything ordered, pre-ordained, they are a different animal from when they separate into individuals who meet us, are thrilled to enter a dressing-room or wait patiently on the pavement for autographs.

Invasion

We are used to dressing-rooms and the bizarre atmosphere of backstage: some of the public will only know it from Hollywood musicals and will have dismissed it as fiction. The fact of it turns some of them to stone. If they don't gush about the show or your performance it's because they are not gushers and are ill-at-ease with semi-naked men and the rush of feet on stone floors, echoing farewells and the crowding of corridors (brushing past half-familiar faces) that is the world of backstage at 10.30 at night.

It is advisable to stay away from dressing-rooms if enthusiasm and even gratitude is not the driving force of your visit. Actors do not want the tensions of social formality at curtain-down. Some of them deal with it admirably (better than ambassador's wives), but unless the glow of pleasure from seeing the show is evident on visitors' faces actors are trapped into a situation of unease which is not of their own making. Criticism of performance or production should be delivered at a tactful time (not while the player is still hot with effort).

Most actors feel committed to a production while they're in it. Circumstances do not always make improvements possible during a 'run' (though one of the great attractions of theatre-acting is the opportunity to do things better). It is frustrating for an actor to be made aware of what might be when he is stuck with what is.

Courtesy

Being polite to our public is part of our job. When people first court us we are flattered, amazed, embarrassed. Then we get used to other people wanting to say hello and graciously accept their attention. Soon we are ducking being pestered: we don't answer fan mail (much fan mail is pathetic, coming from folk with unsatisfactory lives. The nicest thing is to reply warmly. Have you ever written a 'fan' letter? Do you remember the thrill of your hero answering?)

The 'old school' would keep a distance between actor and audience. On the stage we dazzle, in life we may disappoint. Actors and audience don't mix (on hot matinée days you don't share the same lawn). We must keep our mystery, our charisma. Also we must keep our modesty and our energy.

Social Status

Actors enjoy a good deal of hospitality, at the hands of devotees or theatre-supporters or socialite hostesses. The tradition is age-old. Away from home and on a pittance we are glad of good cheer and comfort, drink and succour. Yet we may resent it. Are we second-class citizens? Most of us have a high opinion of ourselves!

Then there is the business of social grading. Where do we fit in? We are put at one end of party rooms. We herd together. 'The actors are come'—'I will treat them according to their deserts' (says Polonius, paradigm of the status-ridden). We don't always have a Hamlet to draw us out, give us the titbits. We stand there in no man's land.

Our life, our calling threatens neat living. Acting seems a vague way of socially connecting. What do we do during the day? (ask ignorant philistines). They assume we're all de-generates. We rove. Where are our wives and children? Grown men wearing make-up! We haven't got two pennies to rub together. Their daughter is all set for Oxbridge too—she'll be led astray!

'In Catholic countries he was refused the sacraments, and an anomalous situation arose by which a man like Molière could be wealthy, respected, received by the king and patronized by the nobility, and yet be buried in unconsecrated ground. Legally even Shakespeare and his great contemporaries were still liable to be classed as rogues and vagabonds, and it was not until the nineteenth-century that the actor achieved a definite place in society, which culminated in the knighthood bestowed on Henry Irving in 1895'. That's from *The Oxford Companion to the Theatre* (a marvellous reference book to our world.)

Hot Flushes

Wait until you're stared at in tube trains, puzzled over from behind a newspaper; wait until people stop you at a bus-stop, poke you like a scientific specimen, mutter, walk away striking their forehead in quandary! 'Don't go away, they say, I'll get it in a minute. George! come here will you? come and help me figure out who this guy is, now wait there.' (They tell you who don't know them from Adam, wish they didn't exist or that George at least isn't as obsessed by your identity as his friend.) They come again. They have it! You were in that terrible play on BBC 2 everyone made such a fuss about. That's where they've seen you before. They knew they had. Their curiosity satisfied, they go away, never to be seen again.

You are left darkling. You are glad you add to the sum of human curiosity, but your ego is slightly wounded: after all they didn't say whether you were good or bad; they didn't really acknowledge that you were an actor, a spiritual influencer of the community; they simply prodded and puzzled over you. They didn't really treat you like a human being. They were bloody rude!

It is our lot. We are public property. We don't realize it, it creeps up on us. We avoid crowds, slink around in dark glasses, wear disguise to travel. You think I'm mad? Paranoid? It's quite possible; but wait until you've appeared in a popular one-off play on the box or a series—wow! and next morning you travel, just like other people, to work, for your ten o'clock rehearsal, on a tube train. It's embarrassing. For everybody. You *feel* important. Voices in your head say Oh! Sod off everybody, what does it matter? Where the hell am I? *Who* am I? Who was I supposed to be last night in that play? I did it a year ago. I didn't even see it!

But they know, your public. You were that thief and murderer, you were that monster. Is it him? they wonder, he look's nicer this morning, nearly normal, but I'll never forget what he did to that woman . . . You get off a station early. You're late for work.

Recognition

Some people would recognize Annie Walker quicker than the Prime Minister. Fame can come upon us unawares. It's not what most of us seek or want. On the contrary we delight in anonymity.

We want ordinariness and extraordinariness in the same amazing frame. We want to go about browsing in bookshops, to sip tea, to go to football matches, to be an unassuming family man, and we want, in our acting, to dream our grand or sordid dreams, be important, make a stir. We're all different, us actors. Some delight in an adoring public, fame, at just about any price. Others hate recognition intensely. Heroes, heroines. Giants. Being loved. (Is that what it is when people cry, 'I love you Elvis'?)

The working actor works. The paraphernalia of publicity, notoriety, exposure of his private life to the world's gaze, these, if they cross his path, he avoids if he can. For the dedicated actor, work is enough, *that* is the public property. His personal pilgrimage through life is very much his own affair. Look at any man's (any person's) life, and if you scrutinize it well it won't, very probably, be an inspiration to posterity! The public and the private, the seen and the unseen, heard and unheard—oh! the mask and the face!

Respectability

Lord Olivier is the first actor/peer. Will Ronald Reagan be the first actor/President? If so it will confirm what we all know; that we all perform all the time, that life is a business of role-playing, and that in playing roles the actor does nothing different from other men.

Actors are respectable if we want to be. Our profession is well established but curiously disordered. Surely we can do better than we do in giving it some cohesion? The danger is that if our Theatre (even perhaps in structure) resembles an establishment, its life is endangered. The English Theatre resembles the wild garden: anything may grow in it. It is unweeded, full of plants choking for lack of organization, but it is wild and can transform, with sudden rain or shine, into miraculous flowering. The function of Theatre is to surprise, above all else. However Michael Billington is clearly right in his exhortations for us to organize the Theatre. Who's going to do it? When?

Publicity

The Press help to sell us and we help to sell them. Stage, screen, radio and TV account for a good deal of newsprint: in some dailies they seem to be the life-blood.

Theatre, reflecting life, contains a cross-section of human types. The Press can plunder the profession and find what they want (from the tit of 'starlets' to the tat that is very much part of the trade). They can interview the sage and mighty, or tell the rags to riches story of Annie Q. who achieved fame overnight after only twenty-three years in Rep.! We are accessible. We want people to know about us. Only when disaster or untold joy strikes citizens in their houses can the 'media' gain access to their lives. Our lives, apparently, are led for the sake of exposure. The Press assume they're helping us when they publicize us. Somebody has said that as long as the name is right there is no such thing as bad publicity.

But notoriety and work aren't always bedfellows. The majority of working actors aren't famous.

Some actors have a gift for drawing attention to themselves. It can be useful. Such people don't usually give a damn.

Businessmen exploit their singularity. Publicity can arouse great interest in individuals, but though you may be able to fool some of the public some of the time, you can't fool directors and producers for very long. Talent will out if it's there: if it isn't— well, you once 'made a splash'. Fame in itself can be a hollow crown. What are you famous for?

The majority of actors prize anonymity off-stage. Acting's their job. Good work, good pay, an undisturbed private life— aren't we entitled to that? Unfortunately our wares must be sold. The paraphernalia of publicity isn't finally about individuals, it's about selling tickets and switching on sets. Only at the peak of the Film Industry does the *type* of publicity accorded to stars really matter; and then it's because they sell more cinema seats than anyone else. Such stars have donated their lives to their public. They have no private life: legends need sustaining. (Fellini's movie *La Dolce Vita* is the classic illustration of the hell big stars suffer. Reporters and photographers stick to their prey like wasps to jam). 'Normality' is fiercely wrenched from such an existence. You've got to be exceptional to stay at the top and not be destroyed.

Journalists

But most of us will never be hounded by the Press. It is perfectly possible to have a satisfactory career and never suffer an Interview or an unflattering photograph even in *Time Out*. But success breeds success and fame fame. We tread a tightrope between exposure and anonymity. We never quite know what will happen. Events make us, more than in other jobs. If you're splashed across morning tabloids you may have less reason to splash yourself across the consciousness of an audience. The true actor (*le comédien*) values 'fame' only in so much as it helps him do work he wants to do; and because people will see it.

Reporters have to sell what they write. They have to present it in a way that will catch a reader's attention if not his imagination. They rarely represent us whole, that's not their job. They make 'news' of us. What they say is as short-lived as our performances. The public demands new 'news' each day.

We are sensitive about what they say, but the majority of reporters are reasonable people. They may want you to vet what they've written, and there is a law of libel: papers are not immune to suffering costs and awards against them in the courts. There are many ways in which we may be written about, depending upon what kind of publication wants us. You may be rung up to provide the odd sentence in a television magazine, or a Glossy may do an 'in depth' article on your love-life. You may be taken to a pub by a busy journalist and in exchange for an unappealing sandwich you will say profound things about Max Frisch or Michael Frayn; or you may be invaded by a reporter and photographer in your bachelor/maiden flat and snapped cracking eggs or operating the waste-disposal unit. It may flatter to have the humdrum of your life thought fascinating. We read the finished piece and are delighted or appalled at our image. We may, though, wonder who the hell they're talking about!

6 Self-organization

The Product

You sell yourself. Half of you has to sell the other half, which you polish and hone like any other marketable commodity. That's why you have to stay at your best come rain or shine, keep fit and ready, head upright, consonants at teeth's ends—you're the commodity you're marketing. (How many dialects can you do? Can you dance? If you had the chance to play Hamlet how would you do it?)

What is your self-discipline like? Do you get up when the alarm tells you to? How many alarm clocks do you have? One reserve in case of trouble? They're an investment!

If we're going to be schizophrenic (and there's a good chance of it) we might split ourselves into two neat halves: the performer and the marketeer (the hustler, the publicist, the secretary, the financial wizard). When we're working we tend to think only in terms of playing our role and are lazy when not being it or working at it. When we're not working we get slack and often lack confidence to persist in altering the situation. Deliberately you must say to yourself: I'm an actor and that is what I have to sell: when I'm not acting I will concentrate on getting or making work, and when I am working I will not forget that I will soon be out of work and that missed appointments or unacknowledged letters will go against me.

If you have a permanent address you can make your 'Admin' life stable. Buy a desk (a table will do, though the surface soon gets cluttered). Why not have an IN tray and an OUT tray? Things to be dealt with, things that have been dealt with. You need files, or one big file (this is an essential professional expense.) A strong file can last a lifetime. Select what you file. If anything, file too much: you'll be surprised how often you want a certain address or have forgotten so-and-so's name; perhaps you want to know what XTV paid you five years ago —are they offering more or less? Say to yourself, will this information be of any use in twelve months' time? If not, get rid of it.

A diary is as important as cleaning your teeth. Keep one permanently on your desk, and one with you. Enter everything as soon as it arises. That way you leave your mind free. The more free you can leave your mind to concentrate on work the better. You'll feel more creative the less anxious you are.

When you're on the move, touring or living away from home, take something like a brief-case to keep your 'business' life in. Scripts, letters, fan mail, railway tickets, pages of reminders for a thousand and one things—keep them compartmentalized; otherwise they'll all be in your head (or out of it) and you'll have far less time to think about work. Efficiency helps you enjoy work. A stapler and a hole-puncher are useful.

All this is only to put a professional aspect on our lives. The same mood of efficiency will spill over into your performing. You'll never be late, you'll know your lines, you'll keep yourself decently groomed (which is only to say you will look employable). Acting is a job, being an actor a profession. Perhaps it isn't important to you—job, trade, craft, business, 'bread', 'getting into' something—what the hell does it matter what it's called? It matters because words influence our thinking.

And what we think of ourselves influences the way others think of us. At the moment actors are casual labour in our society—it's hard to think proudly of oneself or one's job in that context. If we are more estimable we must continually prove it. We must impress upon society that without a healthy *live* Theatre everyone is the poorer. Communities need spiritual communication, man's understanding of man shouldn't take place through books and media removed from real encounter. The Theatre is the lay church. The actor is a priest, Peter Brook has said. Casual labour indeed!

Income Tax

First on the list of every wage earner's 'admin' comes *income tax*. It is regularly the bane of actors' lives (especially Archie Rice's) because our income fluctuates and the tax we pay is assessed on what we earned *last* year. In justice, we should, like writers, be taxed over a three year period (or more): as it is one *good* year amounts to a real headache if it comes amongst lean years. However, it seems quite likely that the Pay As You Earn system (generally in use with employees) will be more widespread soon.

At present most actors pay tax under Schedule 'D' which means that our Income is totted up at the year's end (April 5th is the fiscal date). Our *Allowances* too are totted up (all *bona fide* and receipted professional expenses and those allowances the Government grants everybody). If there is any income left when the allowances are taken away from it, *tax* is paid on the resulting amount: 35 per cent up to £4 500, 40 per cent up to £5 000, 45 per cent up to £6 000, and so on. After about £15 000 it's hardly worth earning anything. *Unearned income* is also taxed with a surcharge. (Perhaps you'd like to know.)

What interests us most are the *allowances*. Every unmarried person can earn £735 tax free. Some allowance is given on Life Insurance and Pension premiums.

Generally allowable expenses, deductible from income, which are wholly and exclusively incurred for the purpose of following a theatrical career (as Equity puts it) are here listed:

Make-up
Hairdressing
Chiropody (for dancers, mainly Ballet)
Theatre laundry
Equity Subscription (compulsory Trade Union Fees)
Tips to dressers, call boys, stage door-keepers etc.

Cost of repair of Wardrobe and Props (if you're a magician?)

Cleaning to Wardrobe and Props (if you're a ventriloquist?)

Cost of replacement of Wardrobe and Props

Cost of renewing Wardrobe and Props

Singing and dancing coaching (including hire of room)

Touring and living expenses, if supporting a permanent home (i.e. if paying rent elsewhere)

Taxis to and from the station on tour

Agent's fees (their ten per cent)

Telephone calls, telegrams, postage etc. (those postcards we mentioned, to remind employers you're alive)

Printing and Advertizements (including *The Spotlight*) *also other publicity*. (According to your taste?)

Photographs, blocks (reproductions and special mountings)

Postage on fan mail (this would seem to be included under telephone calls etc. Perhaps some people get oceans of fan mail!)

Cost of music and Theatre tickets for agents, managers, press etc. (Also the cost of your seat when you go to the theatre: you may be taking over a part or playing it elsewhere? or watching the director's work, or, you may simply be keeping abreast of your profession—like doctors who read the *Lancet*.)

Professional journals—*Radio Times, TV Times, Plays and Players* (*and The Stage, Contacts, Professional Casting Report, Theatre Quarterly* etc., etc. Also certain daily papers are bought only for Theatre Reviews or to know who's won an award or what Peter Hall said about the future of the National Theatre: vital professional knowledge).

That is the end of Equity's list. There are certain other items which may be incurred for *Exclusive Professional Purposes*:

A portion of the cost of rent, rates, heat, light and upkeep of the place where you work (i.e. where you live, probably.

We all work at home as well as at rehearsal. Perhaps more at home).

Certain tapes and records and books. (One is unable to perform Brecht without reading about his 'Alienation' theory. Dialect guides we constantly need. It is very often prudent to hear a good poetry reader before you attempt to become one.)

Professional visits. (The cost of travel to auditions and interviews and meetings.)

Unavoidable travel and hotel expenses (to work and whilst working).

A proportion of the cost of your car (when used on business).

Accountancy. (The cost of an accountant is deductible. You must weigh up the pros and cons of employing one. They are not cheap and they will not do everything you expect them to. They advise and guide you, and they deal, on your behalf, with the Inland Revenue. Accountants are not responsible for the validity of your income-tax return!)

Bank charges.

Subscriptions (a portion at least of the cost of belonging to certain Professional clubs, where work is obtained or devised: and special kinds of physical and professional training must be accounted necessary costs).

What you claim for must be bona fide expenses. You should have proof of them.

The subject of income tax cannot be left without a word of warning. Many of us are, by temperament, prodigal. If we do not save for tax our lives may be made miserable. Actors should always live below their means. Inevitably we are inclined, when the good days come, to spend—perhaps on necessary things; but unless you *save for Tax*, you may be forced into professional situations you would prefer to avoid: some actors had to stay in Hollywood in order to pay tax, even though they hated being there. A common type of actor is one who is generous with himself but mean with money. That shouldn't surprise any of us!

VAT

British Value Added Tax originated on 1st April 1973.

If you earn over £5 000 in a year you are legally bound to register with *Customs and Excise*. If you think you will earn more than £5 000 in the coming year notify them, they are in the telephone directory and their Head Office is:—

H.M. Customs and Excise, VAT Central Unit, Alexander House, 21 Victoria Avenue, Southend-on-Sea, Essex SS99 1AA.

VAT money is not yours: it belongs to the Government; do not spend it: put it in a deposit account. The only money you can deduct from it is VAT charged to you on items that are

The actor and VAT

wholly professional (i.e. your agent's VAT charge, your telephone VAT, your petrol for work VAT (12½ per cent at the moment), your hotel's VAT, your stationer's VAT, your Theatre tickets' VAT).

What is paid to you is called OUTPUT TAX—(what you've taken OUT of the common store).

What you pay out is called INPUT TAX—(what you've put IN to the common store).

If you earn more than £1 750 in one quarter, or
more than £3, 000 in two quarters, or
more than £4 250 in three quarters, or
more than £5 000 in a year, *notify Customs and Excise*.

(If despite your quarters' totals you feel you won't earn £5 000 in all, tell them and you won't be registered.)

Once you are registered you get a VAT number and a quarterly form to fill in. On it you must say what VAT you were paid (you get 8 per cent more for every job), and what VAT you had to spend on Professional matters. You then pay what is left over to Customs and Excise. It may be that they owe you money.

—*If you are not registered for VAT with Customs and Excise you will lose money because you will be charged VAT by other people, but you will not be able to charge it yourself.*

Actors' Insurance

British Actors' Equity Advisory Insurance Service Ltd. is a long-named organization formed in 1972 after efforts by Equity to deal with the difficulties of performers' insurance had failed. Insurance companies think of performers as bad risks for any kind of policy by virtue of the unsettled nature of our work and our unstable temperaments. This generalized view of us has been partly eroded by the Advisory Insurance Service. It has persuaded insurance companies to think more specifically about groups of performers and the different kinds of work they do. It has done wonders: to my knowledge it has reduced motor insurance by more than half.

Their H.Q. is at 131/133 New London Road, Chelmsford,

Essex. CM2 oQZ. Their telephone number is 0245–51581. It is worth contacting them about every form of insurance. They are brokers who will do their utmost to find a company with a policy to suit your requirements (their commission is taken from the company). They are well represented in most parts of the country and they can be seen by appointment at the Equity Office in Harley Street.

Did you know that you can insure yourself in all sorts of ways?

What's the best part of you? You can insure it! Unhappily, though we don't like to think about it, we can too easily become unemployable if we sustain injury or illness. No doubt there will be other things we can do in such unfortunate circumstances, nevertheless our chosen profession might be barred to us. Insurance can at least compensate for a drop in earning power. We can insure the contents of our flat (even if the flat isn't ours). We can insure our belongings when we travel.

Motor Insurance is cheapest through them.

Professional Effects is a policy designed especially for our lifestyle.

Sickness and Accident Benefit. They boast a policy where payments never stop, no matter how long the absence from work. Other kinds of benefit run out.

Pensions Premium. They offer a flexible way of saving for retirement age. You pay what you can each year. You can't touch the money before you're sixty. (You get tax relief on this policy.)

Unemployment 'Resting'

Variety of work is one great privilege we have over other trades. We constantly meet new people, learn new things, attempt new things. Only long runs in the Theatre fix us in a set pattern for some time, otherwise we have the possibility of doing anything, anywhere. Anywhere in the world.

Suppose you've gone to work at a television studio one morning and at ten a.m. you dress up in a dinner jacket and join a crowd of other 'diners' at a Victorian banquet. Cigars are available and bowls of fruit; the champagne is only ginger beer but the speeches are good! What other worker has such a surrealistic morning?

We live in make-believe land: or, to put it another way, we often turn life into what it might be. Ralph Richardson has said: 'Acting is partly dreaming'. Have you noticed how often in Shakespeare the idea (or the word 'dream') appears?

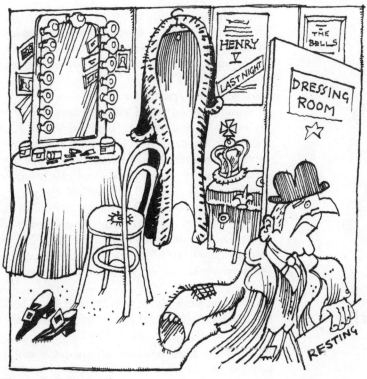

The end of the 'run'

'We are such stuff as dreams are made on and our little life is rounded with a sleep'. That's a view of life that actors, lucky beggars, share more than many.

The price we pay for living with our feet off the ground is not knowing quite who we are or what will happen to us next. At the end of *All's Well that Ends Well* (Shakespeare had a genius for appealing titles) the King says:

> 'The King's a Beggar now the play is done,
> All is well ended, if this suit be won,
> That you express content . . .'

'The King's a Beggar now the play is done'. That is very often literally true!

He who played the King on Shaftesbury Avenue on Saturday night finds himself queuing for unemployment benefit on Monday morning. Unemployment is as much part of an actor's life as employment. The sooner you understand that the better.

The Reality

Here are two examples:

A male student left Drama School at the beginning of 1971. (It's now November 1974.) He worked in Rep. at Sheffield and Leeds; he's appeared at least six times on television; he's made three feature films, and is currently appearing in a West End classic comedy (a great success). He's worked for a hundred and fourteen weeks and not worked for seventy four weeks.

A female student left the same school at the same time. She worked in Rep. at Edinburgh and Chester. She's been in four West End musicals and done the odd TV visual commercial. She says she hasn't 'broken into' television. She has not worked for sixty weeks in over two and a half years.*

Social Security

The first time you report to your local Social Security office, dark glasses and facial hair may alleviate the humiliation. But

---

* *Stop Press*! These two students are doing well in their careers. The girl has just been contracted to play a lead in a television serial (true).

you'll probably be recognized by a friend. 'Signing on' on Monday mornings is quite a social occasion. You don't have to report to your nearest office. Over the years you may pay a good deal of income tax. Don't feel shamefaced about accepting welfare. Single people get £11.10. Earnings-related supplements help too; *but Benefit stops after 312 days.* Thirteen weeks of twenty-one hours work must be done before re-applying. From 6th April 1975 new ways of paying your National Insurance contribution came into effect. They are as follows:—

Class I

Employees (which we are when we're getting paid for a job) will have no National Insurance card. They will have a number, and they must make this known to the employer on starting a job. Earnings of less than £13 a week will have no Nat. Ins. contribution deducted from them. Earnings of up to £95 a week will have $5\frac{3}{4}$ per cent deducted.

Class II

Self-employed people will have a National Insurance card and pay for a stamp. Or they may pay through a bank.

Also they must pay 8 per cent of their earnings between £1 600 and £4 900 (Class IV).

They do not get Unemployment Benefit or an earnings-related supplement or Industrial Injury Benefit (though Equity is fighting this).

Class III Unemployed

You may pay a voluntary contribution (not more than fifty at £2.10 a week in a year). It may be assumed that contributors will benefit when Pension time comes around (at sixty-five).

Class IV

Class II people do not escape this; but Class I contributors who pay income tax under Schedule 'D' (most actors) may be relieved of it:—

To be exempted from paying 8 per cent of earnings between £1 600 and £4 900, get Form CF 359 (from Inspector of Taxes or Social Security Office), *complete it and send it to* Department of Health and Social Security, Class 4 Group, Newcastle-upon-Tyne. NE98 1YU. (This applies to the Tax Year '75/'76 and may apply further.) If in doubt assume you'll earn more than £1,600.

Equity and the Department of Health and Social Security will advise on these matters. The DHSS print explanatory leaflets of all they do.

When you start working, you can get a National Insurance card from your local Social Security Office (or the Careers Office if under eighteen). What you pay (the amounts increase as the cost of living rises) is a contribution towards the National Health Service and your Pension when you become a Senior Citizen.

Your National Insurance contribution also entitles you to:—
Sickness and Invalidity Benefit.
Unemployment Benefit.
Maternity Benefit.
Widow's Benefit.
Guardian Allowance.
Child's Special Allowance.
Death Grant.
Also:—
Industrial Injury Benefit.
Disablement Benefit (but not in all cases).
Death Benefit.
And:—
A Pension.

Keep in Touch

The major problem about being out of work (besides being poor) is what to do with the time. Morale quickly sags. You have to work twice as hard keeping yourself together as you do when you have a job. You may have a fight on your hands—recognize the fact.

We are used to working in groups. It is bad for us to be cut off from people. So, keep outgoing (and going out)—*it is essential not to become isolated and driven in on yourself.* Some solitary spirits don't mind this (some prefer it to the tug of human relationships and the demands the world makes), but for most actors it is not a good thing. One of the reasons for being an actor is the constant contact we have with every kind of human being. When we're jobless we're automatically withdrawn from our natural habitat. Bear this in mind and compensate by regularly seeing friends and fixing up an active social life. Keep abreast of the current theatrical scene. When we're working we often can't see what's going on. Now's the time to catch up on things. (In practice we seem to fall into two kinds: those who want to see shows and those who don't; those who like to keep informed about the profession they belong to and those to whom every show is a busman's holiday and the last place in the world they want to be is the auditorium of a theatre.)

Every day do something that might result in work: a 'phone call, a letter, a meeting—a creative idea.

Home-made Efforts

There's an actress working on her one-woman show. She's been working on it for twenty-three years.

One-person shows are good to work on. There's always the chance of them seeing the light of day, perhaps of hitting the jackpot (Emlyn Williams, Michael MacLiammoir, Roy Dotrice have shown the way). We often have heroes with whom we think we have an affinity—Beethoven? Napoleon? St Francis of Assissi? We know them, we understand them, we even look like them! So all we're waiting for is a script, a way of telling the story, showing the qualities of the person, dramatically, entertainingly.

Max Adrian as Bernard Shaw had not only an eccentric and a wit to portray, but a man whose trade was words. It's almost essential that you have a richness of speech in a one-man show (either from the literary qualities of the subject or the things

115

said about him). Fact and documentation are what they're made up from.

To hold an audience's attention for two hours unaided is a daunting task, the height of egoism. Are you virtuoso enough? Your material must be marvellous and so must your performance. You may ask someone else to research and shape the show (a commission?), or you may combine with them on it. You will need a director, an outside eye to help you. That's essential.

When these things come off they have a wide appeal. They instruct and divert. Children come to learn. You are an actor hero and you have a vehicle that may last.

Two-person shows are also cheap. The past is full of famous relationships. Many people are insatiably curious about the private life of the famous. Perhaps the Chekhov/Knipper letters could be 'staged'? Lovers are not the only duos; there are brothers, sisters, friendships of all kinds.

Three-person shows . . .! Quite seriously a happy blend of talents (including musical ones) on a small-scale is a highly marketable commodity. You can go anywhere and not demand an enormous 'get-out' (the money needed to clear your costs for a week in a theatre).

There must be many extraordinary people whose lives or relationships are worth dramatizing. But you don't have to be someone else, you can be yourself—if you are many-sided enough to astound (like Spike Milligan or Ron Moody).

Poetry

Poetry constantly swims into our ken. We meet it in plays, and who else but actors should get up and 'spout'? On the other hand many people have a prejudice against actors reading poetry. We ham it, dramatize it, and there it should lie, silent and fathomless on the page.

Some people don't want to hear poetry read. They have a case (except that some poetry was written to be said aloud—Hopkins for example, and the Victorians had a habit of reading to one another). Poems are words and words were invented to say. A good poem's indestructible: it will live after an actor's 'killed' it.

approach

In a poem, first of all make sure you know what it means. You can't get up and ramble on regardless. Specific thinking, as ever, gives life to what you do.

Poetry's a compression of feeling in speech. It has obvious forms, clear shapes. Make your effect within the shape of the poem, make the effect the poet has made. All art 'does' something, it has a life. The actor must show the life of the poem. No-one's better equipped to do so.

Everything said by one person to another is a story. So is a poem. Getting to our feet we metaphorically say 'listen everyone', and in the silence we start. We must hold the hearers' attention for the length of the poem (even Don Juan? I hear you mutter), and by the end an 'effect' or 'effects' should have happened, perhaps be left hanging in the air. And what is the story we tell? Whatever the movement of the poem is. With narrative poetry the 'action' or story is clearer than in lyric poetry. The Medieval Ballads for example grew to be 'told' (and Wordsworth's 'Prelude'—an Autobiography, and Charles Causley's 'Ballad of Charlotte Dymond' are other examples of 'stories'); but even Wordsworth's 'Daffodils' has a story of the poet wandering, seeing daffodils, and of what the daffodils do to him; and Shakespeare's sonnet 'Shall I compare thee to a Summer's Day?' has a 'story'—something happens in the poem. The poet suggests a simile of loveliness for his beloved, but then sees it is not apt. He suggests that she can only live on through his poem. In 'I' poems what happens is usually very clear. Work on poems like parts. Through subjectivity we can speak truth and silence those who call us vulgar.

Keats's 'Ode To Autumn'

There's a very useful book called *Understanding Poetry* by James Reeves. In the last chapter he discusses Keats's ode 'To Autumn'.

Imagine you have to read it in a week's time, at an evening

117

of 'Poetry of the Romantics'. You've never seen it before. You know nothing of Keats. What do you do?

You read it again and again and again. You ask people what you're not sure about. Have you noticed that it's written in iambic pentameters—like Shakespeare? DeDumDeDumDe-DumDeDumDeDum. It will help you know that the words 'soft-liftéd'. 'twinéd' and 'barréd' have their final syllables sounded. It will also help you throughout with the movement of the piece. Pay strict attention to the punctuation: it is precise: it always helps the meaning. Do you understand every sentence? The subject, verb and object are crystal clear to you? (The meaning of the poem is not hard for anyone to discover. It means exactly what it says: no ambiguities, no obscure references. The odes 'To a Nightingale' and even 'On a Grecian Urn' are more difficult, and much more difficult to read—especially the former.)

How are you going to read it? As an actor would say 'What am I going to *do* with it?'

What did Keats do with it? We are interpreters. What is the author's intention(s)? Keats is talking to Autumn. So you must talk to Autumn.

That is the simple and yet imperative 'motive' to make the poem live. James Reeves discussing the same poem on Page 183 of his book says many true and enlightening things but he does not say that. Of course he is not writing for performers. He says: 'It is as if Keats, foreknowing his imminent death, were resigned to sharing in the life of nature with its seasonal cycle ending in fulfilment and death'. This is a very helpful clue to the 'tone' of the poem—one of 'resignation'. But an actor could not read three stanzas resignedly without drowsing his hearers into a poppy-fumed sleep! Whatever we do when we read, we must *first* keep the ears of our audience.

Talking to Autumn, it becomes clear from what is said and how it is said that Keats has a relationship with the season. Continually he personifies Autumn. Autumn is a 'bosom-friend' of the sun: the second stanza is made up of Autumn in different 'human' situations—sitting on a floor, asleep, crossing a brook, watching a cider-press. Keats anthropomorphizes Autumn, to show us its different aspects. So must you when you read it.

Reeves's feeling that Keats is resigned to his end will not help us 'animate' the poem. In fact Keats transfers his own resignation into persuading Autumn that it has great virtues, a variety of rich aspects, its own melodies.

'Where are the songs of spring? . . . Think not of them, thou hast thy music too'. Peace, peace, Autumn. Be content with your lot. The tone is one of consolation (only the heavy brooding imagery belies the author's re-assurance). The actor must aim for the positive encouraging tone, and let the imagery do its own work. Keats loved Autumn as he loved the Grecian Urn. The most important quality in a reading of either poem is that an audience should feel Keats's love, which contains humour too. Have you imagined the bees looking up with surprise as still more flowers appear to keep them from their hibernation?

Improvisation

The majority of actors have hidden weapons—other talents, usually undeveloped to the full. Think of the many writers who were or are actors. Writing plays is best learned from being in the theatre.

You're bound to have ideas for plots or situations or just amusing individual lines or ripostes settle in your head from time to time. Many actors write—secretly perhaps, and always unfinished. 'Resting' is the time to gird your loins and have a concentrated bash. Finish whatever you do. Let someone else judge it. Just finish it, unless you do that you're wasting your time.

A lot can stem from improvization. London has groups which meet regularly. Actors come together to provide an audience for each other and encourage each other, also to develop ideas that arise in groups. Should tall trees from little acorns grow, should you be so pleased with what emanates frmo the group that you think more people should have the chance to share the experience, should a viable (in terms of people wanting to see it, paying to see it) proposition emerge, then there are possibilities of help.

The Arts Council

The Arts Council of Great Britain is a body, albeit a human one. It is a non-political set-up for channelling Government subsidy to all the Arts. They have a charter exhorting them to 'promote the knowledge, understanding, practice and accessibility of the Arts'. Without the Arts Council's vision, lack of bias and practical assistance, many of us in the Theatre could have packed our bags long ago. Despite subsidy not keeping pace with inflation, the Arts Council is the prop behind all non-commercial Theatre in the land. It sows the seeds of interest far and wide; it puts 'bottoms on seats'; it brings artist and audience together.

1974 was a year of bitter struggle for the Arts Council. The nation's economy (as we all know) is barely solvent.* 'The Arts' are a minority pastime. Were they going to get enough money to keep the structure of our Theatre going?—they had to forget about innovation. But there are wily heads at 105 Piccadilly: some provision is made to help Experimental Companies (whether on the Fringe or not). Little that is viable (or better still *proven*) will go unencouraged at the Arts Council.

It is not Arts Council's policy to initiate Theatre. They help those who help themselves. They may be useful in putting mutually helpful people in touch with one another. Don't fear to write to them. They have a Drama Department.

Grants

The time for applications for grants is the beginning of November before the year in which you want the money. They will want to see your work and they will want to see your books (to see if you are a financially responsible outfit).

---

* But governments understand the necessity of funding peoples' leisure. Regional Arts Associations span the land.

The Council also spend money on training in the Arts. In the Theatre, in various ways, they help directors, technicians, administrators and performers. The bursaries (gifts of cash for specific reasons) are liable to change both in intention and in amount from year to year. At the moment the Actors' Bursaries take two forms. One is that an actor (with the sponsorship of his theatre director) can be seconded to a Drama School for a period. There he will have a change of scene and professionally influence the place. The quickest way for students to learn is for pro's to take the stage with them.

Actors who have been professionals for at least two years may apply for money to help them get specialized training that will increase their professional worth (dance, mime etc.). You must make out a good case. Your intention must be honest. Apply to the Drama Officer for further information.

Back in your flat, no job to do.

Exercise can be had in a hundred ways. What part of you needs bringing into line? 'The Dance Centre' in Floral Street will keep you fit in a useful way. There's no need to join health clubs and spend money on equipment—unless you want to. The imagination can provide weights. There was a political prisoner who kept fit in solitary confinement, no exercise allowed. He had belonged to a Rugger Club and knew some 'tension' exercises. Have you ever watched Alan Knott playing cricket? He never stops bending and flexing himself, all day long.

Don't drink or smoke too much. You may have heard that before! The thing is you're more liable to get a heart attack if you do, *at any age*.

Diet depends upon your finances. You are very healthy on brown rice, raw vegetables, wholemeal bread and water. (Bake your own bread. It's easy.)

Keep yourself ready. You may be asked to play Hamlet tomorrow. That's the difficult thing, living on a knife-edge; but it can't be avoided. It is difficult, in the hope of your vocation calling, to commit yourself to other pursuits. But you'll probably have to. It's often a question of mind over matter. Worry in itself is entirely unprofitable.

Keep fit and ready for any part . . .

You might like to divide your day up so it doesn't stretch endlessly ahead. Perhaps you can plan a week's activity at a time; but it's better, if you're staying where you usually live, to plan small. Make objectives for yourself (like acting). What are you going to do with the morning? (perhaps the afternoon will take care of itself, a friend will 'phone, you'll meet).

Study Parts

You can read. There's the whole of English Drama waiting for you. It can only improve you professionally.

You can study parts. How well do you know the claissc roles that you are hoping to get your teeth into? You can always 'do' them in your flat. Get them inside you, let them cook in the oven of your gut and the kitchen of your imagination. Good work may be conceived in a bathroom. 'Acting is partly dreaming'. Years hence you will remember a visionary leap that you had making a bed. It might make you the Rosalind of your generation.

Shakespeare's particularly good to live with when out of work. You may not have had a chance to get to know him intimately. Now you can. It's the only way to do justice to Shakespeare—live with him. Only then will you absorb him, make him your own. Make his words your words.

Shakespeare

He was an actor. His characters live through the words they say. It's all in the words. Rosalind speaks breathlessly, joyously. Falstaff dirtily, rhetorically. Fluellen convolutedly, didactically. His characters say what they're thinking and feeling. Put all of yourself into the words. Make sense of them.

Young actors find the Elizabethan and Jacobean dramatists foreign (I've always found the eighteenth-century world of high gloss strange). Don't let the verse put you off. Nobody's more human than Shakespeare.

All Shakespeare's verse is built on five stresses to every line. Five iambs (deDUM, deDUM, deDUM, deDUM, deDUM). 'If music be the food of love play on'.

'To be or not to be that is the question' (deDUM, deDUM,

deDUM, deDUM, deDUMde—that's got a feminine ending).

All jazz is built upon four beats in the bar. If there were no syncopation, no surprises, it would get boring quickly. The same is true of Shakespeare. Like a jazz genius, he rings the changes on the old one-two-three-four-five. Say this like a metronome stressing the long accents (——s).

LEAR: And my poor Fool is hang'd.ᶜ No no no life.
Why should a dog a horse a rat have life
And thou no breath at all?ᶜ Thou'lt come no more
Never never never ᶜ never never.
Pray you undo this button:ᶜ thank you sir
Do you see this?ᶜ Look on her, look her lips
Look there look there ᶜ

EDGAR: He faints. My Lord my Lord.

(That's the death of Lear. Act V. Sc. iii.)
Now say it meaningfully. The stresses might go like this:

LEAR: And my poor Fool is hang'd. No no no life.
Why should a dog a horse a rat have life
And thou no breath at all? Thou'lt come no more
Never never never never never.
Pray you undo this button. Thank you sir
Do you see this? Look on her, look her lips
Look there look there —

EDGAR: He faints. My Lord my Lord.

That's my version. What about yours? The stresses will be different again. Over the basic beat, each Lear improvizes his own solo. You can take a breath only after the c caesura (the pause which may come after two or three iambs) or at the end of a line if the meaning doesn't necessitate running straight on. If in doubt about stress go with basic beat.

You'll have plunged into Shakespeare at Drama School. Most of us touch him at some point. He's the most commercial dramatist we've got. Do you know why 'Macbeth' is called the 'unmentionable'? In the days of the nineteenth-century touring Companies, when business was bad you put on 'Macbeth'. It always did well so to 'mention' it pre-supposes bad business. If you quote it in a Theatre, forfeits will be exacted.

Money-Earning Tasks

Being unemployed, have you got to earn money? Here's a list of jobs—cleaning houses, offices; driving; secretarial; typing; teaching (most people can teach something); supply teaching (if you've got the necessary qualifications); shop assisting; decorating; removals; modelling; writing (have you ever tried a short story? They're always in demand. If you've got a writing bug follow it up. Try any avenue to sell it. Literary agents will help you); window cleaning; baby-sitting; washing-up; waiting (in eating-places); cooking (hire yourself to rich friends); the application of any skills you have (hair-styling? physiotherapy? horse-riding? dancing? singing? playing a tea-room piano?)

Don't sit in your flat all day. That's inviting misery. Unless there's someone there!—you may have good reason to remain indoors.!

The Telephone

You don't have to be on the end of your 'phone. If you have an agent you will keep in touch with him of course (don't ring him twice every day, he'll see you coming and duck), but don't nail-bite and ponder the insultingly silent invention of Alexander Graham Bell. Ask a friend or relation to sit-in if you expect a call. You can pay the G.P.O. (£20 or so a year—£5 a quarter) to intercept and transfer calls to where you are or where someone is.

Telephone Answering Services may be found in *Yellow Pages*. The most enterprising seem to be ANSWERING LTD. Cost is about £25 a quarter with slightly reduced rates for performers. You can use them as a telephone number if you haven't got one, or you can use them as an alternative number (when you're out). They will answer your 'phone from their office, or the G.P.O. (interception service) will transfer calls to them.

You might want to invest in a telephone answering machine.

A tape-recording tells callers you're out and records messages. Several people might share one machine. Contact the G.P.O.

A Sense Of Purpose

Your life will change according to how long you're without work. No-one can live very long on hope. The way to remember you're an actor is to act, and though it may seem odd, don't only do physical and vocal exercises daily but play parts as well. Go the whole hog, alone maybe, in your room. *If you were acting on a stage you would burn a lot of energy playing a big part—eight times a week. If you can somehow find ways of doing the equivalent you will be wise.* Play favourite parts or experiment, but stretch yourself; why not play all the great parts you can think of? If you can put in four hours a day thinking and performing, you may, with a light heart, spend the rest of the time as you wish. *But your prime aim is to discover work somewhere in the British Isles. Or make it.*

Marriage

'He that hath wife and children, hath given hostages to fortune; for they are impediments to great enterprises, either of virtue, or mischief,' says Sir Francis Bacon in an essay called 'Of Marriage and the Single Life'. It's true of actors. for those who build a wall of material security around their family may not furnish them with emotional happiness, and those who shine at the latter might have difficulty with the former! It's not so much a matter of families preventing us performing great exploits (in the way we see them) as the fact that great exploits will be performed (given the slightest opportunity) however many wives or children we have. The ambition of an actor is blatant.

But the actor's lot—his independence, his travelling, his uncertainty, make the family hearth a pleasant prospect. It represents a warm island in a cold sea. And the roles of breadwinner and father are attractive ones.

One cannot pronounce upon the requirements of the human heart. There are no better dads than actors. They respond to their children in ways that more conventional chaps don't. And

126

love, of husband and wife, has been what men have lived and died for. But acting threatens. It makes fierce demands: takes us away when we are needed and keeps us domiciled when we should be in the world (for often the actor is at home during the day).

It's tempting to say that no actor can be easy to live with. The phlegmatic consistency of the so-called 'family man' is not the quality of personality people come miles to see (though often actors live a kind of Jekyll and Hyde life,) stage and home fulfilling different aspects of the same person).

An actor's home is like a pilot's landing ground and the experience of marriage and fatherhood deepens one's emotional reservoir. If you find a soulmate strong enough to endure the haphazard life well and good.

Last Word

People become actors for all kinds of reasons, all kinds of motives, which they may not understand until they have long trod the path. Glamour is a strong pull of course: the 'house of illusions' casts its magic beam and our lives seem dull by comparison. When we're young we admire actors, they are our heroes and heroines. Their beauty, grace, wit, strength or compassion conquer us. Actors seem to have power over other people. They are talked about a lot. We think it would be splendid to be so admired ourselves.

A passage in Thomas Mann's *Felix Krull* describes the shock of seeing a performer backstage (old and ugly) after being mesmerized by him onstage. Actors are you and me, people— 'fed with the same food, subject to the same diseases' as others. It is tempting to say that every illusion must have its corresponding disillusion. Certainly our 'art' is hardwon, and the mystery of our trade is offset by difficulties, discipline and the desert of no-work which surrounds us.

The further you go into being an actor the further you go into yourself. The same analytic instinct which makes mechanical engineers or psychiatrists goes to form the inward-looking actor. And yet nightly he must be a shining extrovert!

Fulke Greville, Lord Brooke, wrote these famous lines in the sixteenth-century:

> Oh wearisome condition of humanity!
> Born under one law, to another bound.
> Vainly begot and yet forbidden vanity.
> Created sick, commanded to be sound.

Whether the actor is created more sick or more sound than anyone else is not the point. What is certain is that he is an artist in this respect: he knows the deep pains and sometimes the triumphs of creation.

Perhaps actors have themselves to blame for how much their lives are dictated by other people—employers, planners of theatres, directors, producers, all sorts of people pronouncing upon their work and meddling in their lives—who certainly could not begin to survive as performers themselves. We shouldn't always save our voices for the show, they should be heard wherever and whenever our dreams and livelihoods are concerned.

If actors took as active a part in professional matters as they do in other areas of human dilemma, our prospects would be more cheerful than they are. Witness George Murcell's new 'St. George's' theatre in Tuffnell Park, London. A fifteen-year-old dream realized through determination, belief and sweat.

Postscript

The national council for Drama Training has been established as a result of the Gulbenkian Committee's inquiry. It comprises: an independent chairman, six representatives from Actors' Equity, six employers' representatives (Theatres' National Committee, BBC, ITV etc.,) six representatives from the Conference of Drama Schools, and *observers* from the Department of Education and Science, local authorities, further and higher educational establishments with particular interest in Drama, and the Arts Council. (Are *any* of those working actors?)

The NCDT will concern itself with the size of the training sector, financial support for Drama training and in-service training, and *recognition of certain schools (rather than others)*.

Going on the Stage is a booklet of the Gulbenkian committee's findings. It is essential reading for anyone contemplating a performer's career.

Appendix—names and addresses

The Actors' Company, 1–6 Falconberg Court, London W1V 5DG

Answering Ltd., 16 Jacob's Well Mews, George Street, W1H 6BD. Tel: 01–935–6655

Arts Council of Great Britain, 105 Piccadilly, W1V OAU Tel: 01–629–9495

Association of Community Artists: Maggie Pinkhorn: Tel: 01–240–0301

British Actors' Equity Association incorporating The Variety Artistes' Federation, 8 Harley Street, W1N 2AB. Tel: 01–636–6367

British Actors' Equity Advisory Insurance Service Ltd., 131–133 New London Road, Chelmsford, Essex. Tel: 0245–51583

BBC Radio Auditions, Drama Department, Broadcasting House, Portland Place, W1A 1AA

British Film Institute, 81 Dean Street, W1V 6AA. Tel: 01–437–4355

British Theatre Institute, 9 Fitzroy Square, W1. Tel: 01–387–2666

Calouste Gulbenkian Foundation, 98 Portland Place, W1N 4ET

Childrens' Theatres—see *Contacts*, for individual managements.

Conference of Drama Schools—see *Contacts*

Council of Regional Theatre (CORT), Mercury Theatre, Balkerne Gate, Colchester, Essex. CO1 1PT. Tel: 0206–77006

The Dance Centre Ltd., Studios, Costumes, Productions, 12 Floral Street, WC2. Tel: 01–836–6544

Greater London Arts Association (GLAA), 25 Tavistock Place, WC1

G.P.O. Sales: The General Manager, Sales Division, 151 Shaftesbury Avenue, WC2

Independent Broadcasting Authority, 70 Brompton Road, SW3. Tel. 01–584–7011

Independent Theatre Council: Graham Devlin, 14 Forthbridge Road, London SW11

Independent TV Companies Association, 52 Mortimer Street, W1N 8AN

Institute of Chartered Accountants in England and Wales, Moorgate Place, EC2. Tel: 01–628–7060

London Theatre Council, 19 Charing Cross Road, WC2

The Musicians Union (National Office), 29 Catherine Place, SW1. Tel: 01–834–1348

National Youth Theatre of Great Britain, The Shaw Theatre, 100 Euston Road, NW1. Tel: 01–388–0031

Personal Managers Association, 91 Regent Street, W1

Roundel, Multi-Media, Redan House, 2 Redan Place, W2

Stage Management Association, 81 St. Mary's Grove, W4 3LW

Writers' Guild of Great Britain, 430 Edgware Road, W2 1EH

Further reading

The Actor and his Body by Litz Pisk, Harrap, 1975.

The Actor's Ways and Means by Michael Redgrave, Heinemann, 1953.

Advice to a Player by Denys Blakelock, Heinemann, 1958. Compacted of wisdom but dated now.

Dictionary of the Theatre, Penguin Books. Beware, by the way, the punctuation of Penguin Shakespeare!

Disruption of the Spectacle (5 Years of the Fringe) by Peter Ansorge, Pitman, 1974.

Methuen University Paperbacks have a splendid list of books on **Drama**.

The Modern Actor by Michael Billington, Hamish Hamilton, 1974.

On the Art of the Theatre by Edward Gordon Craig, Heinemann Educational Books, 1968.

Oxford Companion to the Theatre, O.U.P. Third Edition, 1967.

The Professional Casting Report, Jaguar Books, 3 Carlisle Place, SW1.

Samuel French in Southampton Row is the specialist Theatre bookshop.

The Set-Up by Ronald Hayman, Eure Methuen, 1973. An authoritative picture of our trade.

The Stage, published weekly, is the British profession's only newspaper. Motley but intriguing.

Theatre Quarterly, T.I.E. Directory, *Alternative Theatre* etc., TQ Publications, 44 Earlham Street, London WC2.

Understanding Poetry by James Reeves, Pan Piper, 1965. Heinemann Educational Books.
Voice and the Actor by Cecily Berry, Harrap, 1973.